Untangled

Stories & Poetry from the Women and Girls of WriteGirl

Also from **WriteGirl Publications**:

NOTHING HELD BACK: Truth & Fiction from WriteGirl

PIECES OF ME: The Voices of WriteGirl

BOLD INK: Collected Voices of Women and Girls

THREADS

LOOK AT ME LONG ENOUGH:
Creative Writing from the Girls of Destiny Academy

Untangled

Stories & Poetry from the Women and Girls of WriteGirl

WriteGirl Publications

Los Angeles

Untangled: Stories & Poetry from the Women and Girls of WriteGirl

Executive Editor: Keren Taylor
Editors: Abby Anderson
                       Phoebe Brauer
                       Tracy Chait
                       Allison Deegan
                       Jen Dohr
                       Kate Gale
                       T. Faye Griffin
                       Erica Kelly
                       Cece Peri
                       Teresa Rochester
                       Marlys West

Art Direction: Keren Taylor
Book Design: Sara Apelkvist
Cover Art: Mixed media assemblage by Keren Taylor
Cover Photography: Thomas Hargis
Printing: Chromatic, Inc.

FIRST EDITION
Printed in the United States of America
ISBN #: 0-9741251-4-8

Orders, inquiries and correspondence should be addressed to:

WriteGirl Publications
Los Angeles, California
www.writegirl.org
info@writegirl.org

When things are terrible, write. When things are great, write. Write all the time.

Acknowledgments

To all of the **girls of WriteGirl**, thank you for bravely articulating your realities and your dreams in these pages. We asked a great deal of you, and you gave back more than we ever expected.

To the **women of WriteGirl**, thank you for your enthusiasm in building this community. Through sharing your insights, skills, and experiences as writers, you have encouraged us all to believe that scribbles can become masterpieces, that shy can turn bold, and that words can make magic.

To the **Editorial Team**, thank you for sifting, sorting, and polishing the work in this book. We know it was more than "just one more late night" and we thank you for hanging in there!

Phoebe Brauer, thank you for everything that you contribute to WriteGirl and all our publications and projects. And thank you for keeping me laughing even when the sky seems to be falling.

Erica Kelly, thank you for collecting and organizing all of the author submissions and releases and for so gracefully keeping up with our brisk pace.

Allison Deegan, thank you for keeping the big picture in all our minds, and for helping with every detail along the way.

Sara Apelkvist, you have done it again. What a fantastic environment you have created for all our authors in this book's unique design. Thank you for your care with every word and every sentiment.

Community Partners, we appreciate all your professional guidance and support.

Yucca Community Center, we thank you for giving us the space we need to write and thrive.

Wasabi, the chocolate lab, thank you for all your warmth, wags and slow blinks.

Jacques Taylor, thank you for all your wisdom, patience and encouragement. You remind me to breathe, you keep my feet on the ground and you inspire me to keep searching for what eludes me. Thank you.

– Keren Taylor, Editor

Untangled

Table of Contents

Chapter 3: Obscure Mathematical Formulas (School)

Chapter 4: True & Loyal, Fiercely So (Friendship)

Foreword

A girl's voice, a woman's voice – the gift we come with, ours to use if we are not afraid, if we protect it and nurture it and let it howl, in joy or pain. This is the gift of WriteGirl, to help the girl's voice not get lost and thereby help the girl not get lost.

It is by our stories we women know ourselves and our strength and if we don't get those stories out, we are half-whole, half-silent. In the pages of this anthology you hear young women talking about everything: beans and rice, the color of their skin, sisters and brothers. They play with language, throwing words up in the air and onto the page with honesty and exuberance. You can feel it, that excitement of girls learning to use their voices – in fiction and nonfiction, in poems and fragments of memoirs.

I fell in love with WriteGirl when I attended one of the monthly workshops, a crowded, noisy room full of girls and their mentors writing together, laughing together, heads tilted towards each other, heads tilted over paper. That's the genius of the program: matching high school girls with mentors who are professional writers and having all of them, pros and non-pros, write together – so it's more than just a mentorship, it's a creative partnership. To watch them all at work, to be in a room full of scribbling females, is thrilling.

Not all of the girls will go on to become writers, at least professional writers. Some will; some won't. But all of them will carry the idea that their words matter, that they have a say, a stake, a right to be heard. That, of course, is the ultimate gift of the program.

I am very pleased to introduce this volume, to join – for a moment – the exuberant WriteGirl community.

Anne Taylor Fleming

Anne Taylor Fleming is a nationally-recognized journalist whose work has appeared in many publications. She is an on-camera essayist for the NewsHour with Jim Lehrer *and author of a new novel,* As If Love Were Enough.

Introduction

This is WriteGirl's fifth season and fifth anthology. What a journey! The organization has grown tremendously. This year, amongst our newest group of college-bound girls are several of our original members who joined WriteGirl in the eighth grade. Now, all these confident young women with specific aspirations and distinct voices will leave our community to join another, bringing with them all the openness, optimism and critical thinking skills they have acquired.

In five years, we have quadrupled our membership, we have expanded to South Los Angeles, we have paired hundreds of girls with professional women writers and we have produced countless writing workshops and events.

Five is an interesting number, a number of balance. We have five oceans, five digits, five elements and five senses, and here are five ways you can use this book:

1. Find out what's on the minds of women and girls. You'll laugh, you'll think, you'll wonder.

2. Keep it by your toaster. You can enjoy a poem or short story in the time it takes for your toast to pop up.

3. Write with us. Throughout the book, you'll find writing tips from our members to inspire the writer in you, as well as a whole chapter of writing experiments from WriteGirl.

4. See how different writers approach the same theme or experiment.

5. Get a glimpse into the process of writing – on every page you'll find a comment from the author about her inspiration.

Creativity isn't an instant acquisition. It needs to be nurtured and nudged into existence. We've seen that something special happens when you bring women and girls together and give them time and encouragement to express their ideas and emotions. It is a completely unique environment from home, school, work or even a writers' room. I am always uplifted after a WriteGirl workshop or event, and we hope that you can share in some of that spirit through this anthology. The girls and women of WriteGirl live challenging, exciting, diverse and resonant lives and we are thrilled to share them with you.

Keren Taylor
Editor

Chapter 1 { Identity }

Pour Me Off The Edge

I don't know what the alchemical magic formula is in writing, but I think it has to do with voice, the transformative power of voice.

What you are scared
of in your writing,
you are scared of in life.

Follow the narrative path — sentence after sentence — to discover who you are.

I write to get what is good and brave and strong inside me.

How to Become a Writer

Stephanie Almendarcz, age 18

Three things inspired this piece: reading lots of poetry at the library, dreaming of becoming a writer, and feeling helpless after dropping out of high school.

I look at Sandra Cisneros' *House on Mango Street*, and Gary Soto's *A Summer Life*, and I want to be like those characters, stuck in a summer life, eating melon on Mango Street, finally having a house for my family and me. I know we all deserve more than this. My mother deserves everything — a backyard with lemon trees for barbeques and hammocks, a garage to shelter us from the rain when we throw parties. If only I could get things going. If only I could be a writer someday, but I feel like I'm going nowhere. And I'm barely on step one. Don't have my G.E.D. yet. Crying on steps like these. Falling lives with autumn leaves. Crying for a summer life on Vernon Street.

Now we're not on Vernon Street anymore and not eating melon on Mango Street, either. No lemon trees, but at least we have a pine tree. Don't have a backyard, but we have a porch. We don't own this house, but it's home, sweet home. We have a garden now with roses so red you can hear them laughing, like my sister, my mother, and I. We're so alive, finally. Not a writer yet, but I'm eager. Finally got my G.E.D. Not crying on autumn steps anymore. The leaves are growing and green. Past step one, but another one's got me. That's okay though, I've got my keys. And I've got this moment, this house and this chance that's passing — like a blindfolded shooting star.

Rebel Yell

Lena Brooks, age 17

To start, let me start with:

I am so quick to love

the grass, the green, all sheets of sun.

And I am all poured out all over,

bare my lips and teeth in devotion.

The world is holy, really holy and

I put all my faith in the world,

even with its broken windows,

there is bright light in the cracks.

And I rattle and roll in the face of deformity.

And I shake brittle bones on the heels of acceleration,

velocity, and the Holy Ghost.

I am just born in the World-Our-God.

I need all these matters of strength to

pacify me in my explosions.

I am bursting with the stuff of love.

Everything creaks and I think about

the rhythms of mixture, everyone busted and lovely.

Who will break me just a little so I fit the gaps?

Yell and yell and yell and be held.

And here we have established such important facts:

that my love is dripping from the trees,

that my love is the sea, that my love is

jellyfish because I sting and sting,

get up, get rash, get long and love and die,

that I need a net for all of me,

and make my breaths for all of mine.

I'm Nadine

Nadine Levyfield, age 16

This was a WriteGirl warm-up where we had to write the first things that came to mind. I discovered a lot about myself.

I'm Nadine. I love fruit snacks and my pals and lying on the grass and Japanese fast food and inside jokes and piggyback rides. I like deep voices and cold hands and being barefoot. I make a lot of lists so I don't get lost. I love to order the kid's specials at restaurants, but I wish the portions were three times bigger. I'm the kind of girl who falls in love with someone I've never seen before if we lock eyes in the middle of a crowded hallway. I will stand outside the house of the boy I love singing loudly in an attempt to serenade him, only to find out that he's not home. I'm not very good at reading maps or anything involving algebra, and I find myself doodling excessively and staring at the clock during math class.

Sometimes I think high school is the biggest waste of time in the entire world. I think I would go crazy if it weren't for lunchtime and my friends and journalism. I love looking at old, faded Polaroids and at the trippy, colorful shapes and intricate designs inside kaleidoscopes. I still love getting tucked in, especially when someone I love does it. I like to take walks and people-watch, not knowing where I'll end up or if I'll find an adventure. I think models are beautiful, but I'd rather look at ordinary people with flaws like scars and freckles and bruises because they are unconventionally beautiful.

My ideal afternoon would be spent wandering the aisles at Amoeba or browsing the thick stacks of books at a used book store. I wear turquoise eyeliner every day and buy most of my clothes at thrift stores and make most of my own jewelry. I love staring out the window and looking at the trees and listening to songs on repeat that mean something to me. I am constantly making mixed tapes for the people I love. I love indie music, even though I can't play any instruments, and lately I can't stop listening to Spoon and Pixies and Built to Spill. The world stops when a song I love comes on the radio.

Fireball Explosion

Cydney Neal, age 13

I am fireball fuchsia.
I am a young girl
with big dreams.
I am a happy person with a wonderful family.
I'm sure you have one, too.
Even if you don't think so,
there is something special
about you.

One Atom

Devon Regina DeSalvo, age 16

So I was thinking, we all want to be somewhat normal, but if everyone were normal, would we all get bored and want to be insane instead? Then, if we were all insane, would our insanity be considered normal? If so, we'd live in a world full of crazies and oddballs. Oh, wait — we already do. We all go around saying, "Oh, so-and-so is so normal," but I bet when you're not looking, that person's favorite thing to do is run around and bark like a dog. Everyone has some craziness. It may only be one atom, but it is there whether you accept it or not. We are what we are.

16 Ways to Be a 16-Year-Old

Aisha Holden, age 16

*My mentor, Wendy, suggested I try a fu[n]
assignment from her memoir class: direc[t]
someone on how to be you. I was forced
to examine myself. I learned that
I definitely need more sleep!*

1. Monday through Friday you must wake up at 6 a.m. to get ready for school.
   But don't actually get out of bed until 7 a.m. (mind you, school starts at 7:56).

2. Wish you weren't in school until 2:08 p.m. when school is over.

3. Only feel liberated when swimming every day after school.

4. Avoid doing homework for as long as possible. Laze around, listen to music,
   play solitaire on the computer.

5. On Saturdays, sleep in until noon (on a good day) unless there is a WriteGirl
   workshop or meeting.

6. Hang out with friends or family, sometimes wishing you were in bed asleep.

7. Go to the movies and eat popcorn you will wish you hadn't.

8. Go back home and watch "Saturday Night Live" or a rental movie your dad picks out,
   which is surprisingly good.

9. Don't fall asleep until around 3 a.m.

10. Secretly hate Sundays.

11. Avoid doing the laundry, so do homework.

12. Avoid doing homework, so do the laundry.

13. Finish homework and laundry, then work out. (Workouts only happen on good days.)

14. Watch "Extreme Makeover Home Edition," "Desperate Housewives,"
    and "Grey's Anatomy."

15. Go to bed around 11 p.m., but don't actually fall asleep until midnight because
    you still have some homework you kind of didn't do.

16. Start all over again.

How to Be Me

Wendy Tigerman, mentor

Talk to strangers, talk to your computer, talk to yourself. Try to shut up just a little bit. Celebrate the mundane. Eat in your car. Dream of liposuction. Thrill at the color of eggplant, the texture of roses, the light at dusk. Wipe your nose and your mouth on your sleeves. Lay on top of your dog. Rub lavender on your husband's moustache. Build a shrine to attract money. Keep secrets. Hug freely. Buy shoes you can't afford. Be envious and competitive. Be generous, loving and forgiving. Try not to keep score. Own eight-weeks worth of expensive panties. Go commando. Clamor for attention and cringe when you get it. Pay for a gym membership but never ever go. Try not to collect things. Collect small toys that make obnoxious sounds. Worship your son. Let goooo of your son. Be an atheist who prays a lot. Laugh long and loud, easily and hourly. Be compulsively self-revealing. Love the smell of wet cement, chlorine and salt air. Drop names, dislike most poetry, avoid foreign films. Share your struggle so that others are comfortable with theirs. Have a flexible IQ.

Nappy Hair

Tajsheena Curtis, age 14

I wrote this piece at the Creative Nonfiction Workshop where we talked about groups we are part of.

I love my hair.

It can be braided, nappy, fried, died and laid

to the side and everything else.

I could put it in locks, I could wear it up,

down, pressed,

relaxed, kinky, my roots showin'.

Anything you can think of, my hair can do it.

Although sometimes it can be hard to tame

and it can go back to black

so that everyone can see my kitchen, my nap naps,

and my beady beads.

I still love my hair no matter what.

When I'm Sad

Kamaria Holden, age 13

When I was in third grade we had to write a poem about being sad, so I looked back at that poem and worked on it more.

It's not a pleasant feeling, being sad.

When I'm sad I feel like a rock that has never

Been picked up.

I've never been thrown around like the other rocks have been.

Even people who collect

Rocks never pick me up.

Why? Because I'm too sad.

Just sad,

Broken in two buried under

Other rocks.

But now,

I'm on top

And not broken

In two.

It's a day when the sun is shinin' and nothin'

Can stand in my way.

I'm finally

Being picked up

And held

And loved.

On this day, I am

Happy.

A-N-G-E-L

Deborah R. Bramwell, age 16

Cliché feelings make me blush —
but they are
Things like
I want to read Bruce and Havel
Stand out — fit in.
I want
Escape.
Home.
I want to be cold
and excited
and true.
I wish I spoke of normal things instead.
Did it for myself because I wanted to
Not for attention
Envy's a dirty thing
But a deeper blush —
The details
I want to be beautiful —
Sure —
In lime green tights
just like Wilson Jermaine Heredia.

I Am Black

Chianti Morgan, age 16

I am Black. Nappy hair black. Thick lips black.
Curves and his black. "Black power!" black.
You see I am black. A beautiful Deep Dark Chocolate Black Child.
But believe it or not, I used to not be beautiful
black for a very long while. I used to be burnt black
Charcoal black. "The lights are off can't see where you at, ha! ha! ha!"
Black.
These names that were given to me made me feel sad
Because I knew black was beautiful
But being this dark was ugly, was bad
I always knew as a young child that I was going to have challenges
Because of my race
Because of my skin
But even with my African-American Brothers and Sistas
I couldn't fit in
Because again, the shade of my skin
And so I listened to the devil whisper in my ear
Making me cry. Convincing me that I didn't belong here.
Many times I went home feeling like walking dirt.
Jumping in the shower, washing my skin so hard it made me hurt
More
My parents always told me I was pretty
They knew it was true, but I knew that's what parents
Were supposed to say and do
Now I'm laughing with my friends for a little while
And here comes this lady with a beautiful smile
"Your skin color is sooo beautiful!" she said to me.
She admired it so much it was almost kind of creepy
From that day on my "friends" started acting shady
But I knew it was just 'cause they was hating
And then I found that during the time I was
Hurting, crying, and thinking I was ugly
There were these fellas who were checking me out
And trying to get to know me
But I never noticed. And do you know why?
Because I was too busy paying attention to the haters
And the devil's lies. But now, now I pray to God
And always thank him with a smile
Because I know that I'm a beautiful
Deep Dark Chocolate Black Child.

Into Green

Keren Taylor, mentor

I read an article in the newspaper about using plants to clean up toxic industrial sites. I loved some of the words in the article and I remembered a WriteGirl experiment where you take a few unfamiliar words and create a poem around them.

I will pour myself into a small glass

You will bring the glass to the edge of an abyss

lift the glass

toast silently

pour me off the edge

so I can fall

fall fall

back into the earth

seeping through mud, rocks, roots

like electricity into a grid

until I am sucked up one day

into green

shot back into existence

in a completely different molecular order

phytostabilization

my toxic attributes

hyperaccumulated into a thousand leaves

harvest them

discard them

keep the straight stalk of me

I am remediated

contained

I can't hurt you now

Dust

Noemi Cabrera, age 15

I was going through some hard times because of the loss of my father and I wrote a lot, including this poem.

I'm falling into that space again
Where everything rolls away
And I become dust

Dirty, unwanted, light dust
I am taken from every home
And put into a new place I don't want to be
Always carrying something new with me

I am unable to stay in one place, even unwilling
Just as dust is shut away from the world
Going on unnoticed, yet troublesome
So I'll go on that way

On my own, upon my mantelpiece
Unnoticed and alone

identity

Days of Emotions

Lindsay Martinez, age 14

Boring Monday

Playing with my thumbs

Biting my fingernails

Rolling my eyes

Twisting my hair

Staring off into space

Tapping my foot

Humming to myself

Happy Friday

Smiling with excitement

Laughing

Serious with wonder

Curious about plans

Overwhelmed with party invitations

Relaxed that the week is over

Thankful I don't have to wake up early the next morning

Thinking of what lies ahead for the weekend

Calm Sunday

Waking up to the bright morning sunshine

Tasting the sweet scent in the air

Dancing towards the bathroom

Staring out at the ceiling skylight

Enjoying my Calm Sunday

A Meditative Moment

Alix Pham, mentor

This was inspired by a series of books by the well-known Indian Bhagwan named Osho.

In the long exhale of life
and the long inhale of life,
the smell of loud birth and quiet decay
permeates the tapestry.
In the pause of each breath,
the divine illuminates
moments of the simple ordinary.
In the silence
of my still, empty mind
I am full of light.

Rush

Paloma Elsesser, age 14

The wind is blowing in my dark brown hair,

which lay down for once.

My mocha skin meshed with the colors of the wind

like long skinny fingers being pulled through my knotty hair,

tears falling from my eyes rush into the strong air

giving me goosebumps against my thin dress

simply imprinted.

Cold Coffee

Melani Sutedja, age 17

My mentor, Amaree, and I were at a local Starbucks trying to find the perfect subject we could both write about. Of the mass of eclectic Los Angelenos, I picked the plainest Jane (at least, The Grove's version of one), just to see where it would go.

Her almond eyes are fastened to the stark, black ink of her Amy Tan novel. Nothing, not the bald-headed woman with the hoop earrings or the scruffy bearded waiter eyeing her, can distract her. Someone that sounds like James Blunt comes onto the radio, and I try to make a beautiful poem or a long-winded story about her, but her impression eludes me as quickly as her almond eyes drown behind the edges of her paperback.

The aroma of milk and macchiato lingers in this LA coffee shop. "An Americana," the waiter yells, gesturing to the Starbucks coffee cup in his hands, and I realize the voice on the radio is a woman, not James Blunt. The waiter gives up, and approaches her with a napkined cup of espresso in his hands and a smug look on his face. "Your Americana, ma'am," he grins and walks away. She blushes an Estée Lauder blush as she scurries to leave her mahogany seat, but little does she know, she leaves the napkin behind with his number on it.

Old Benjamin McGuire

Vicki Biegner, age 16

This piece was inspired by an old man sitting at the Swork coffee shop one day when I met with Shannon, my mentor. He was the most peculiar man there, and I thought he would make a great character.

Old Benjamin McGuire sits at his laptop one Sunday afternoon. He wrinkles his nose, which emphasizes the worry wrinkle on his forehead, and adjusts his outdated glasses. His stringy grey hair that has not been washed in weeks is tied back in a ponytail. He lives alone in a bachelor pad in West Hollywood, but recently came across the trendy town of Eagle Rock, overflowing with coffee shops and martial arts studios. Not a big fan of the martial arts, Benjamin chooses to spend every Sunday at Swork, hoping to gain the courage to ask out the cashier, Lisa. He used to work as a business manager for Johnson & Johnson, but was recently let go when he was caught stealing office supplies from the supply room.

Now he works part time at a gay bar in Silverlake and is hit on constantly. Nobody knows about his new lifestyle, and he continues to hold up the façade that he is still a successful businessman by wearing a nice shirt and tie and pretending to do serious work on his laptop. Really he is playing Pac Man trying desperately to get his name on the high score list. He never has and probably never will. Every Sunday he comes into this coffee shop on the corner, sits down at the table nearest the counter, and orders three drinks just to have an excuse to talk to Lisa. His first wife left him for a college student she met when she returned to school for a bachelor's degree. It has been six years since then and the only date Benjamin has been on was a blind date where he was set up with a professional wrestler named Thunder Bolt. Needless to say, it didn't work out. So here Benjamin sits every Sunday sheepishly hoping Lisa will notice him and be the one to make the first move.

He fell in love with her the first day she asked him, "What can I get for you?" and has been having dreams about her ever since. His brother Pete is a private investigator and looked up this Lisa as a favor to his little brother. Some might classify this as stalking, but in the unconventional home Peter and Benjamin grew up in, this was normal behavior. Benjamin doesn't like to recall his childhood, but it was anything but average. He witnessed his mother kill his father when he was two, so he grew up with his deaf grandfather. He grew up alone and never learned any social skills, a classic loner. Benjamin will spend the rest of his life coming to Swork, pretending to be something he's not, trying to impress Lisa the cashier, who secretly wants to become a nun.

The Man in the Blue Shirt

Aisha Holden, age 16

Aisha's mentor, Wendy Tigerman: Aisha really went "undercover" to do this assignment. She borrowed my huge sunglasses to avoid being seen as she observed the man in the blue shirt.

The man in the blue shirt is pacing around Starbucks as if he's waiting for someone, or something. Food, perhaps. Maybe a seat? Couldn't be. There are a few open places. He stares up at the menu before circling one more time. Finally, he places his order, and he knows exactly what he wants: Café Americana with coffee cake.

His cheeks are like Marlon Brando's in The Godfather, and he even has that same scratchy, mafia-like voice. He's wearing light brown sunglasses with gold trim, light enough that you can see his eyes. They're the faded, watery eyes of a man who's lived a long time. His hair is grey, almost white, with evidence of its original color. There's a patch of gleaming baldness at the back of his head. But his arms are hairy, almost wolf-like.

The man in the blue shirt adds everything available to his drink — cream and sugar and even honey. He does this slowly; he's in no hurry. While he fixes his drink, he looks around as if looking for someone. He finds no one. Then he walks slowly back to his seat with his head down. Perhaps he's looking at his food. Or maybe he's sad that he will be eating alone. Again.

His seat is off in the corner, in the back of the café. He takes his time before sitting, setting his table. He takes off his glasses and scans the café one last time. Abandoning his search, he sits down and begins to eat, but not before carefully adjusting his blue shirt.

Shadows

Fahiya Rashid, age 14

Shadows
What are they?
Our opposite twin.

They are our gift from God
Letting us know that we are never alone.

When we are down,
they are always there to bring us up.
When we are up,
They remind us not to be too high up.

They are Black and White
They are Dark and Light

Shadows
What are they?
Our opposite twin.

I wrote this poem by combining lines from several different pieces.

Chutes & Ladders

Gabriela Cardenas, age 17

Now that I have switched sides

I dare myself to turn the tides

I wonder, what can a single person do

Though sometimes he may feel the same

There is no joining of souls, no fusion in passion

(Though those are the rumors

That everyone bothered to learn)

One person is still one person

With her hopes pinned to the ground

And her cries of mercy a ligament to skies of ignorance

Conceptions and theories have no place

Because, obviously, there is so much more

To this pilgrimage than it lets on

I cannot have faith

In that which is without a limit

Inconceivable red rivers of life

It is just a simple roll and the luck's run out

Chutes and ladders but it's all chutes for me

Sliding down the long snakes

I find myself at the start again

Chapter 2 {Family}

Spit That Out

Fiction

*Tip

When you write get into it. When you
~~see~~ feel like your bored your stories
will be boring. Make your story wake -up.
Dont kill it and put it to sleep!

Use humor, irony, and melodrama, just don't abuse them.

Hands Linked Together with a Bowed Head

Corie Coleman, age 16

Silence at the dinner table, quiet and still

Hands linked as one, bowed heads

Eyes closed while Auntie Jo blesses the food

Brother's stomach's longing

Cousins in front of grandma's porch

Lights on automatically

Playing ball unaware of the keen thorns

That protrude out of the cactus — a poke

Rivers of cries flowing from black eyes

Sprinting in the house to my mom

Panicked, wondering

Where will she find anti-bacterial and bandage

Uncle John assisting Grandma Louis in the kitchen

Pop, pop, popping of fried chicken grease

The lizard peeping in, searching for where it belongs

Auntie Marilyn painting a red, fierce color on her toenails

Tai and my daddy burp, then return back to silence

At the dinner table quiet and still

Hands linked as one, bowed heads

Eyes closed while Auntie Jo blesses the food

Changes in Love

Julia Guest, age 17

I noticed the drift between my sister and me as we started to live our separate lives as teens. I led a section of the Poetry Workshop using this poem as an example of how one thought can trigger so much more just by continuing to write.

May 1990
Twin flowered dresses
We sang united off tune
Two sisters wanted the best for each other and nothing more

Let me teach you how to whistle
Let me braid your hair
Let me love you
My little doll

Bathtub frenzies
Sharing toys
Giggle hysterics no one understood
We lived in the same imaginary world
Together forever we said, hand in hand

September 2003
Competitive rage
The need to be better
She copied me — the phrase has a new meaning
Our worlds, images inside our heads have changed
We're different, but the same
It was you, you, you
Now it's me, me, me

Rice and Beans

AJ Reza, age 14

Rice and beans
Rice, fried with chicken stock
And oil, mixed with garlic and
Tomato sauce

Long grain rice, carefully
Fried and mixed with
Tomato sauce and a
Healthy dose of laughter

Flock to the table
Prayers said
The first words
Pass the rice and beans
Plop of rice
Plop of beans
Mix
Take out the bacon (grimace)
Added for flavor
Laughter, peals of it
Grandma's specialty
We are rice and beans people

Crickets Don't Chirp in Torrance

Karly Abreu, age 15

I have a unique relationship with my brother. He's my very best friend. This particular piece was inspired by a depressing Saturday I had. My brother got me out of bed at 2 am.

Our weekend is over

The night is cold

Ocean breezes tearing in

Nothing to say

The silence speaks

All the words in a language

Our movie quotes cannot.

And this is nothing new.

My dear friend,

I think I understand.

That Night

Vicki Biegner, age 16

The little girl curls up in the corner of her room holding her hands to her ears as hard as she can to block out the yelling. She is too young to know what is going on, but she can grasp the fact that Mommy and Daddy are fighting again. The front door slams and tears run down the girl's cheek. Mommy is gone again and now Daddy is the only one home. He is mad and when he is mad, there's reason to be scared. Usually he takes out his anger on the little girl and even her littler sister, but tonight the fight is really bad. The girl goes to hide under her blanket. Her sister doesn't understand what is going on. After what seems like decades later, the door slams again. Now Daddy is leaving, too. Two little girls sit in their room, alone, scared, and confused.

The little girl has grown into a teenager. Mom and Dad are on good terms again. They went to marriage counseling or something, but as long as they stay together to give her a spoiled lifestyle, she couldn't care less. She is no longer the bewildered little girl she had been that one night. She is grown up now; ready to break away from the protection of her parents. One day her greed gets the best of her and she goes snooping in her mom's sock drawer for money. Instead of money, though, she finds a letter that was never mailed. Curiosity convinces her to open the envelope. Reading it, she wishes she had not. The words "he loved another woman" will forever stay embedded in her brain.

Now the teenager is driving home from college. She is going to surprise her parents; she got an A in her American Literature class. She pulls up to the house where she grew up. Nothing has changed, and yet something seems different. A waterfall of memories, both good and bad, comes rushing back. She turns her key and enters her home, but nobody is there. She puts her things away in her room and starts to watch TV to kill time, but gets restless. Later that night, her mother comes home. She doesn't look so good. Her eyes are puffy, as if she had been crying for the last few hours. The girl takes her mother in her arms, rocking her back and forth. She knows her father has finally left for good, never to return. A mystery that began to be unveiled when she was just a little girl was unfolding fifteen years later. What had started that one night was finally over. It was the end of a painful journey but also a new beginning.

family

47

Spook Night (An excerpt)

T. Faye Griffin, mentor

As a comedy writer-producer and former stand-up comedian, I've spent an inordinate amount of my adulthood behind-the-scenes in comedy clubs. This is an excerpt from my latest play.

AT RISE: FLETCH AND NADINE
ENTER THE MAIN SHOWROOM OF
"FLETCH'S HOUSE OF LAFFS."

FLETCH
We're not going to make it.

NADINE
You're going have to stop and
talk about this sometime!

FLETCH
Not now, Deenie.

NADINE
Fine! I'll wait until you're
on a cold slab, with a tag
dangling from your toe.
Better?

FLETCH
Which toe?

NADINE
Dad!

FLETCH
What? I like the left big
toe. The right, I'm not so
crazy about.

NADINE
Dad!

FLETCH
Nadine, stop being a nudge
for a minute, will ya? Set
the tables.

Fletch flips a light switch
near the bar. The lights
flicker before going out. He
gives the wall a swift kick.
The lights come on full force
like a beacon.

NADINE
This place is falling apart.

FLETCH
What are you talkin'?

Fletch and Nadine shield
their eyes. Fletch kicks the
wall again and the lights
tone down to normal.

FLETCH (CONT'D)
Voila! Like new.

NADINE
Can't you see what this
place is doing to you? You
don't sleep. You don't eat.

FLETCH
True. I haven't had a decent
meal since Gloria passed on.
God, I loved that woman.

NADINE
She didn't "pass on." She's
working for another family
in Florida.

FLETCH
Leaving me alone with your
mother and her cooking.
That is until she passed
on. God rest her.

NADINE
God! Dad! You know Mom's
not dead. Come on, say it
with me, "My wife is alive
and living in Palm Springs."

FLETCH
All right. My wife is alive
and living in Palm Springs,
with my ex-business partner,
the ratfink, in a twenty three
hundred square foot fake
Tudor, that I paid for, mind
you.

NADINE
That's a start. Now say,
"The club is losing money
and should shut down."

FLETCH
What happened to my little
princess? You used to believe
your old dad hung the moon.

NADINE
It's over, Dad. One good
night isn't going to make any
difference.

FLETCH
Not true. In 15 years with
your mother, I had only one
good night, and look what I
got for my trouble — a wonderful daughter who is going
to get out of my hair and set
the tables.

NADINE (deadpan)
I'm pregnant.

FLETCH
What?! Are you nuts? What
are you doing to me? Who'll
help me around here?

NADINE
Okay, I'm not pregnant.
But what if I want to get
pregnant? Or move to Paris
and become a chef? Or a
sidewalk artist?

FLETCH
I gotta tell ya, Nadine —
and I mean this from the
heart — those drawings you
used to bring home from
school? Awful. And let's
not discuss your cooking.
Suffice it to say, you take
after your mother. Stick
to waitressing.

NADINE
I can waitress in Paris.

FLETCH
You'd leave me to run the
club by my lonesome?

NADINE
I'm just a glorified slave
around here, anyway.

FLETCH
Oh well, everybody's got
to pass on sometime.

Afternoon Coffee

Stephanie Allen, mentor

This piece came from an experiment in the Creative Nonfiction Workshop in which we wrote about a photograph. I chose a photograph of an older African-American man, salt and pepper hair, dressed in an open collar shirt and sports jacket, resting his chin in his hand, a "to-go" coffee on a table in front of him.

These afternoons when I just get to sit and stare are well earned after decades of toil, raising my kids and keeping debt to a minimum.

My daughter is staying at home these days having given birth to my granddaughter, Kismet, a few months ago. Bettina and I didn't get too much time to ourselves when she was growing up, with me working and her going to school and dance class and then the boys. Man, there were a lot of boys. Now we get these afternoons when she takes Kismet for a walk and meets me for a coffee. We talk about Bettina's plans to fix up her house — something I like to help out with. I go over with my toolbox for a few hours and do my handyman thing. We talk politics and write letters to Bush and Time Magazine and Bettina emails them from her laptop computer. We both like to read biographies. The latest was about John Coltrane. I blow a little sax myself from time to time.

There she is. She's stopping to adjust Kismet's hat 'cause it's slipped down on her face. I get choked up when she bends over and tickles Kismet's toes and kisses her puckered lips. I'm a rich man.

The Bicker of the Century

Lindsay Martinez, age 14

This piece is inspired by my parents. When I wrote it, the story sounded like a script. This scene stems from a specific experiment on moving the story and the characters forward through dialogue.

HUSBAND
Before we start this, let me just tell you . . .
this is, like, my room. You hardly ever come in
here.

WIFE
Okay, okay, I know.

HUSBAND
Yeah, you say that now, but as soon as I make one
simple suggestion, you'll go into another one of
your hysterical fits.

The wife rolls her eyes and sighs deeply.

WIFE
So, you're going to start with the walls, right?

HUSBAND
I was thinking a dark green.

WIFE
On all four walls?

HUSBAND
Well, five, if you count the ceiling.

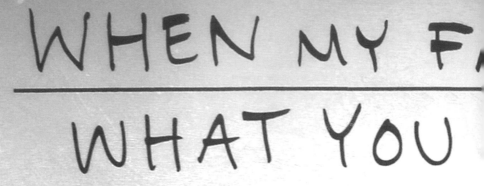

WHEN MY FA

WHAT YOU

At WriteGirl workshops, we cover the walls with posters. Each poster features a prompt based on the theme of the day. During lunch, sharpies squeak across white paper taped to the walls.

mother & stepdad

ILY CELEBRATES,
AR IS...

When my family celebrates, what you hear is...

- My mom's cackling laughter and my sisters yelling at my dad for cheating at Dominos

- My mom, grandma and sisters all trying to speak over the others' loud voices

- Loud Reggaetton music

- Loud Italians telling stories I already know

- Very entertaining political arguments

- VERY LOUD Mariachi music

- German cusswords in a crescendo of laughter

- Pasta slurping and tales of old

- Spanglish, laughter, and cries of "Grandma, you work too hard!"

- Silence as everyone gobbles up mom's delicious one-of-a-kind meals

- Clanking of utensils on china plates

- "Mom — did you burn the cookies?"

- Gospel jam session

- Load Reggae and even louder voices

She's Not My Girlfriend

Hansanii Frazier Williams, age 14

The knowledge I received from the Poetry Workshop helped me write and edit this somewhat satirical poem.

In public
Sometimes I kiss her
She hugs me
Or puts her hands around my hips

We walk together
Holding hands

In restaurants
She'll feed me and I'll feed her

I look like I'm 19
She looks like she's 25

But when we are together
People stare and frown at us
Do they think we're lesbians?

I don't know why
We love each other

She carried me for nine months
Gave birth to me
She's my mom

The Old Man Visiting

Allegra Calderon, age 18

My mentor, Karen, and I decided to write about a specific place we had been in the past, but put fictional characters in it. We were recalling times we each had visited Hawaii. We discovered we had probably been to the same beach, but had very different experiences.

You'd expect that being away from the main city, it wouldn't be this loud. Waves crashing, that's normal. Dead air, normal. Sun beating, burning, normal. Child crying, two children crying — that's not normal. That's what draws my attention to the young girl. She gets annoyed, tries to bribe them with a sandwich, cookies. Frustrated, she runs toward the water. The children are left helpless, can't follow her. They can just sit and watch and absorb, and soak it in. I sit and watch. Sunrays, sunscreen, sand, and infinite sand. Hands move swiftly, sand sticks to me. I try to differentiate this sand from others I've felt. The young girl comes back as if to have found some relief in the water. I can't watch any longer; the children depress me. They send me back to the old questions. Where is she now? I wouldn't know, I couldn't say. She playfully tickles the kids to convince them to take her offer, and she finally wins. They take the sandwich as if to squeeze some last bit of nutrients into their adolescent bodies. I wipe off the sand, but there's no point, it sticks. Apply a patch of sunscreen, lay the towel down, sit down, no, get up, get up. But it's not so easy anymore. Maybe these old bones can find some relief in the water. I take a dip. I float, paddle. She's still sitting there with the kids, takes photos, laughs, wears sunglasses, and Mom and Dad come out. So serene, so happy, so picturesque. If she'd never left I could have had that. I could have had them. I float, bob in the water, swim towards the break.

Odysseus Follows

Deborah R. Bramwell, age 16

I love The Odyssey for the story, but I am always distraught when Telemakhos disappears, so I tell stories about him and how his life must have been.

EXT. BEACH – DAY

Odysseus enters, looking a little too proud and very angry.

ODYSSEUS
Telemakhos, what is wrong with you? You leave without telling anyone. Your mother is worried sick.

TELEMAKHOS
But not you? Do not mock me, Father. My mother knows well that I can handle the island. Twenty years is a long time.

ODYSSEUS
Stop this foolishness, Telemakhos. Come back inside.

TELEMAKHOS
Thank you, but I misbelong there. Please look no more to my coming.

Odysseus is furious, half with himself.

ODYSSEUS
What right have you to issue orders?

TELEMAKHOS
May not the lowliest peasant beg?

ODYSSEUS
Of course. Of course, a peasant may beg, but you, Telemakhos, are a prince, not made for begging.

TELEMAKHOS
Then I am made for ordering! Or perhaps to you, my superior, it is fit that I should beg?

Odysseus knows he doesn't have that kind of smarts. He's clever in situations, not with words.

ODYSSEUS
Come inside, Telemakhos.

Telemakhos wanders a little, stoops to pluck a flower.

TELEMAKHOS
No, I am happy here.

Odysseus advances toward him, but catches himself and stops.

ODYSSEUS
What is it you want from me, Telemakhos? I came out here to find you.

TELEMAKHOS
I did not ask it. And it is unso. You came out here to find the son we both wish I could be. Please stop looking, Father.

Telemakhos turns to
Odysseus for the first
time.

TELEMAKHOS (CONT'D)
Please stop hurting yourself
this way.

Odysseus looks stunned.
He cannot speak. For a long
moment, Telemakhos watches
him, then dusts off his
hands and begins walking
away. Odysseus calls after
him, desperate.

ODYSSEUS
I did not tell you go,
Telemakhos!

TELEMAKHOS
Yes, Father.

Telemakhos stops, walks
to the edge of the stage
and sits, legs dangling
like a child. He plucks yet
another "flower" and begins
tearing off the petals.
His lips move, murmuring
to himself.

ODYSSEUS
(reluctantly)
Telemakhos . . . will you
not just come inside, damn
it? Telemakhos . . .

TELEMAKHOS (aside)
I am Tem to Mother. I am
Tem to the swineherd and
goatherd. Mother said it,
when I was small. "Tem
who rides the waves," she
would say, and until he
came home again I never
understood . . . I do
not think I understand
now. I do not ride the
waves. I do not leave,
do not return . . .

Snacks

Gabriela Cardenas, age 17

My mom was not the kind of mom who got up in the morning to pack lunches for my sister and me. We were responsible for either packing our lunch the night before and putting it in the refrigerator, or, if we'd forgotten to do that, making the mad dash around the kitchen in the morning, throwing whatever we could find into Ziplock baggies before running out to catch the bus. Ours was not a well-stocked pantry. I found out later that this was not because my mom wished to deprive us of snacks, but because she was afraid she would eat them all.

My grandma always said
speak slowly and clearly
because there might be old people in the audience.

I wrote this piece at the Character & Dialogue Workshop. It was awesome to make two boys fight about clothes.

Clothes Don't Make the Man

Dinah Coronado, age 16

INT. ADAM'S BEDROOM - NIGHT

ADAM, self-conscious younger brother, confronts SAM, his cool older brother.

ADAM
Sam, you're wearing my clothes again.

SAM
You let me borrow them, Adam.

ADAM
I let you borrow them a week ago. You can't just take my stuff whenever you want.

SAM
Yes, I can. I look better in them than you do.

ADAM
You look fat in them.

SAM
Adam, relax. I'm not going to hurt them.

Adam gets more and more worked up. Sam laughs at his brother's distress.

ADAM
Just take the clothes off, right now!

Sam chuckles.

SAM
Dude, we're close, but not that close!

ADAM
Ha, ha. So funny.

SAM
I need these clothes. I have a date with Sonia.

Adam is shocked.

ADAM
Sonia from next door?

SAM
Yeah. She's hot, huh?

Adam is outraged.

ADAM
I told you I wanted to ask her out!

SAM
You couldn't handle her, little brother.

ADAM
And you can?

SAM
Better than you.

ADAM
That's it. Take off my clothes right now!

SAM
Make me.

ADAM
Mom!!

Sam shakes his head,
disappointed.

SAM
Mom, Mom. The little mama's
boy. Sonia is not for you.

Adam accepts defeat.

ADAM
Whatever. I can't believe
you would ask her out
like that.

Sam softens a little.

SAM
Fine, I'll take off the
clothes. But I'm still
going on that date.

Nineteen Years

Susan A. Kitchens, mentor

I began by writing down the date, March 8, 2005, and counting back the years since then, considering them this way and that. After hearing someone else's story at a WriteGirl reading, this piece tapped me on the shoulder and said, "Finish me."

Nineteen years ago, they died. Not long ago, I drove to the house. Tucson's dry air wicked away moisture, evoking long-ago sounds and smells. I saw visions of the crystal doorknobs, and the hexagonal bathroom tile, and the fat porcelain propeller faucets. I heard the mantle clock. It whirred behind a thick adobe wall of memory. And chimed. Do the people who now live there know what happened?

Nineteen: that's how old I was when Grandma entered my bedroom the morning after her son's funeral. She said, "I don't think I'm a good Christian. I don't know if I can forgive what happened to him. Oh, my boy…children shouldn't die before their parents." Thinking back, my heart sinks. I failed her. I said, "God says to forgive. He will give you strength." She nodded, as though taking my words to heart. Today I know the words I wish I had told her then: forgiveness isn't a matter of being a good Christian, but a good human. But I had no real words, only lock step "trust the Lord and have faith" words — words that squelched the deepest and truest thing my Grandmother had ever told me. I was young; I had no sense of what it means to bury your own child.

Today I say, "Grandma, I'm sorry I failed you. I was only 19 years old." Nineteen years ago today you breathed your last. Three months before, I came for my cousin's wedding. Dad, too. I watched in your bedroom as you put on your earrings. "I'll wait in the back room," I said, and turned and stepped through the door. Crash! You cried, "Oh, honey!" I rushed back in, alarmed to see you crumpled on the floor in the corner. "Aspirin," you said, "On my dresser." You gulped the pills down. Dry.

Dad called for an ambulance. While we waited, you shook your finger at me. "Just wait, this will be my fault," you said, your head twitching toward the other room where he, Grandpa, sat. The previous night, with gall in your voice, you described the trees out back that you loved. He had cut them down.

Three months later, you got up early. And fell. Again. We don't know much. But we know enough. My uncle knows too much. Grandpa called him. Six o'clock in the morning. "Your mother fell. She's gone, and by the time you get here, I'll be gone, too." It wasn't until the day after they were lowered into the ground that I managed to ask where their gunshot wounds were.

Nineteen years is enough time for a girl to be born, grow up, get religion, and echo know-it-all drivel from the shallows of her un-lived life to her grandmother. It's been a long time since I've wept for you, Grandma. Colors have leeched out of the memories, and the spiky red horror and scribbled shock have faded from your passing. Today I weep for the 77-year-old woman who lost her son. And the 19-year-old girl who could not comfort her.

The Place

Sarah Vance, mentor

My dad spent his boyhood summers in the sheltered companionship of his four older brothers at a lakeside retreat in northern Michigan. Under the branches of tall fir trees, the big white house was built on a strip of sand that became his place. "The Place," he called it. When I was fifteen, my family was living in Detroit, but my dad had left his heart at "The Place," and we spent the summers there. Dad was devoted to the upkeep and maintenance of a battered old wooden sailboat, which according to family lore, he'd bought for two hundred bucks from a guy who'd been using it as a planter for petunias.

Dad didn't have an easy time getting his brothers out on the lake anymore. David and Dudley had moved out of state, and Roger spent summer vacations at his in-laws' cottage on another lake. That left Phil, who lived right next door. Phil didn't like to be rushed. One spring weekend, Dad came north hoping they could work on the boat while it was hanging dry dock, only to be informed that Phil would be tied up all weekend doing his income taxes. Dad was sympathetic, until he learned late on Sunday afternoon that Phil was struggling with the 1040-EZ form.

I hated being trapped on a boat in the middle of the lake with my dad. He was always barking orders at me. "Comin' about!" he'd yell. And he'd be oh-so annoyed when I didn't instinctively duck and get out of the way of the boom. And so, Dad spent most of that summer waiting for Phil, but he didn't seem to mind. He'd patch holes in the sails, rake the beach, and putter around in the shallow water. And some days, just as the sun made long shadows of the trees around the lake, Phil would appear at the top of the hill. Dad would bundle up the sails, tuck them under his arms and wade out to the boat. He'd hoist the jib and have the little boat gathering speed in a late afternoon breeze by the time Phil hit the beach. My dad's sense of humor was cutting and dry, and Phil's infectious laugh seemed to burst from him like an operatic aria. As the boat tacked back and forth across the lake, their companionable laughter would be carried across water that was now streaked with vivid shades of gold and bronze sunlight.

I spent the summer waiting, too. Standing impatiently on the shore, gesturing wildly and pouting dramatically until they returned. So I could beg a ride into town, in order to roam the gift shops in search of toe rings, incense and cute boys.

Dad died six years later, right after I graduated from college. Phil died two years after that, and the sailboat went to auction soon after. I miss them all. I miss "The Place." And now I wonder what I was waiting for.

Christmas Struffoli

Shauna Smith, mentor

We never make it anymore, Christmas Struffoli
"Too much work, too many calories," Mom says,
but I think perhaps it is because it reminds us
of the holidays we used to spend with family
we no longer see.

It was a spectacular dessert, culinary architecture,
that the three of us made together,
mother and daughters,
only for Christmas Eve.

Fragrant, warm, honey syrup
drizzled around
and around a mound
of marble-sized puffs of fried dough,
like tiny golden tree ornaments
piled fifteen inches high
into a towering cone of spun sugar.
Decorated with multicolored candy sprinkles,
it was an edible miniature Christmas tree
sparkling on my mother's mother's cut crystal cake stand.

I miss pulling apart the scrumptious gooey clumps
of honey-soaked pastry,
but even more, I miss the family
that no longer gathers around it.

55th and Keeler

Marietta Putignano King, mentor

I was reminiscing about visiting my grandparents' pizza place in Chicago every Sunday when I was little.

Aroma

Fills the house with the

familiar family flavor.

Secret family recipe

Tasty, tangy, tempting me

to blow my diet yet again.

Takes me back to five,

Tricycle terrorist in the

pizza place.

Loving hands show me how to

flour and roll, flour and roll

A cheesy, steamy kiss.

Unknown

Joan Watson-Patko, mentor

I still have some unresolved issues with my estranged father that I try not to let interfere in my life.

Don't know how to feel,
Not sure what to say,
Would you recognize me?

Never knew me,
Haven't seen or spoken to me,
Does it even cross your mind?

Didn't need you,
Turned out just fine without you,
Do I want to know you?

Have your memory in my mind,
Not sure as to its authenticity,
Would this change it?
Will I recognize you?

Sorry to hear you're sick,
Never wished that on you,
Call back in another 20 years.

A Warm Bed

Jennifer Dohr, mentor

*I had read Rolf Jacobsen's poem about an ant walking
in the F imprint of a Firestone tire on a country road,
and I was inspired by the structure of the poem.
His, as does mine, begins with a specific setting, and
then a character is introduced and set into motion.*

A blue morning in September 6 a.m.

The bed still sweet and softened

By warm sleepy breaths.

She stretches her lithe arms, her narrow back follows

Blonde hair lifting and falling gently on her down pillowcase

(the one with the pink roses she picked out of the magazine, age two).

I don't know when I knew she was with me

At 3, when she stumbled in, a soft "Momma?" on her lips?

At 4, her strong legs wrapped around one of mine

Like a boa claiming its prize?

Or now, as the sun, too, groans while she

Climbs her pulsing body into mine?

Birth is a betrayal.

I know now this much is true.

family

My Stepmother

Monika Zoltany, age 17

My stepmother is delicate
Refusing when I try to include her
In my tropical world
Outside our cavernous home

Four Days

Allie List, age 15

Mommy came home last night
To a house without a daddy
Somber silence fills the air
Joined by trash that hasn't been taken out
In over four days
Overflowing trash just like the tears
On Mommy's and Daddy's kids' faces

Sometimes Mommy tries to hug them
But she keeps forgetting they're even there,
Not because she doesn't love them
It just doesn't seem fair

Daddy, why'd you have to go?
Pearly gates offer more
Than the front door

The phone calls keep coming
No one understands
Mommy and her babies
They just want daddy back at home
To take out the trash
Wipe off the tears
Squash the spiders and fill his role
But he's buried six feet under

Ever since you died
All I've wanted
Is for you to come back
And a cigarette

My mentor, Fielding, asked me to write a revenge poem, so I did. It is about my mother, who happens to love this poem.

Snip your Hair

Devon Regina DeSalva, age 16

I'll snip your hair

Cut it all off until you look like a man

I will replace your weight loss bars with bars to make you gain

I will cut your credit cards in half

I will shrink all your clothes

Every trick in the book I will try

I will give all your shoes to the dog

I will do it all

Crazy is where you will be driven

Off a cliff you will want to jump

Then when I am all done

I will look at you with big doughy eyes

And I will say I am sorry

But I have my fingers crossed

There Are No Such Things as Chairs

Marlys West, mentor

My mentee, Lena, and I were doing a writing experiment where you create a list of titles, select one, then write the poem that goes with the title. I didn't expect that this particular photograph would come to mind.

Lonely, brooding, the kitchen table, too short to be put
to good use now, and the ottoman robbed of its better
half is now bitter, feuding with the coffee table who
has always had the couch and notices nothing missing.
In the natural world there are rocks for sitting by the
bright green duck pond where my daughter picked up
and ate discarded duck bread, white and brown. What
does it matter that ducks are dirty creatures? What of
Avian flu? She bites the bread with her two lower
teeth and gums, one top tooth almost poking through
but not yet touching what should have been the ducks'
breakfast. How good the world must look to her, white
bread in dirt for the taking, ducks for the watching and
chasing, the kiwi-fruit-colored water in the manmade
stream carrying away all spoken warning; *spit that out*
splashing in the catch pond. Bread swallowed & gone.
I can't remember my father ever sitting. There's one
color photograph of him with a cat in his arm, sofa a blue-
green bird, leaf and vine pattern behind him. It's not
yet 1974. Brown sweater and beard, black and white cat's
limbs out like a dowser's split rod, my mother's flash-
bulb burst reflected in both sets of wide-open eyes.

Chapter 3 {School}

Obscure Mathematical Formulas

This piece was inspired by an incident that occurred with a girl at school.

Backwards World

Taylor Gray, age 16

Calm, cool and collected

The bell rang

The scent of freedom grazed my cheek

Like a newfound love for coffee

I closed my locker, pressing against the cold metal

The glide in my stride broke

A serpent's eye glared, then stared

Brushing my shoulders

I buried my pockets in my hands

My lip bit down on my teeth

I was walking forward in a backwards world

warily waiting

to weaken

well-versed wiggle-waggle

The more I moved forward in this backwards world

The more my tears flowed

The more my nostrils flamed

She hadn't gotten the memo

So due to my forwardness in a backwards world

I spoke her a letter, put a stamp on her forehead

And mailed her mouth to Mars

Bored

Noemi Cabrera, age 15

I'm going color-blind
The hues and the very essence
Of my surroundings
Drip away from my fingertips

My thoughts become static
Almost distorted
All he's doing is talking
Just talking

I'm trying to drift off
Into another world
Yearning for something to happen
It doesn't seem to be working

Time itself is stopped
By this man's endless speech
And we are the silenced victims
Of his unearned authority

Scribbles on a paper state his title
Which almost anyone could claim
There is no proof of life in the room
Everything is still and quiet

I feel a murderous pain
In my temple, a pulse, a throb
I'm still waiting for something to happen
Anything would do

Slowly but surely, this is driving me insane
Still talking, just talking
Does he know we aren't listening
That we've lost the will to care?

This treacherous silence
Is fatal to my active mind
Bringing my thoughts and imagination
To their knees

Just when I think I'm about to snap
Give in to the madness
Threatening to consume me
The bell rings and we are detained no longer

Tenth Grade

Nadine Levyfield, age 16

She woke up on the wrong side of bed. She had been up late and had tossed and turned for hours. She has told her parents over and over that she has insomnia, but they don't believe her. Her whole body was sore, as if she had slept like a contortionist all night. She pushed away the blue and white polka dot sheets and warm covers and slowly got out of bed. She pulled on the same rumpled clothes she had worn yesterday because she liked her new skirt with the little hearts and her soft turquoise sweater from a successful trip to Goodwill. She pulled her hair into a messy bun and ran out of the house, cursing under her breath, hoping she wouldn't be late.

She walked-ran the two blocks to school, passing the traffic as it began to rain. She looked down at the thin, cut-off tights on her pale legs. She was never dressed appropriately on cold days. She ate her fruit snacks in homeroom like always and quietly worked on maps in History, while the other students laughed and talked and had their palms read by a cool substitute. The rest of her classes were a blur; she was so tired and already sick of high school, even though she was only a sophomore. She didn't care about the French Revolution or limiting reagents or multiplying matrices. She just wanted the day to end.

The rain let up by fourth period, but the sky was still grey and full of clouds, looking like it could split open any minute. The mindless chatter of her friends at lunch made her want to meet new people. She stood under the tall oak tree and stared at her shoes while they talked about the things girls think about when they're in high school: intercepting secret love notes and memorizing their crushes' class schedules and developing alternate routes to class to see them. She watched the cheerleaders performing a cheesy, clumsy routine on the quad to the school band's pathetic polyphonic ring-tone rendition of "Love Shack."

After lunch, she tried to drown out her teachers and wished she were somewhere else. She watched the second hand of the clock move, minute by minute. She doodled in her notebooks, which were covered in treasured song lyrics and crowded clusters of drooping flowers intertwined with obscure mathematical formulas. Suddenly, she noticed that the sun was coming out. It was shining brightly in a radiant blue sky. To her, this beautiful day was wasted at school. She should have played hooky, taken a blanket to the park to lie down, stretch out, feel the warm sunshine on her face and grass in her hair. She wanted to take a walk not knowing where she would end up. The bell rung, shaking her out of her daydream. She started home to finally get some sleep.

Lunchroom

Karly Abreu, age 15

I sat down at the blue lunch table with the sunken top and uncomfortable seats.
The people I sat with I actually don't talk to anymore — go figure — after
spending 7th grade together, only knowing each other from the other side
of a blue lunch table. I stared hard at my thin, styrofoam tray. I had a slab of
lukewarm, grey funk (it could pass for hamburger meat, if it had actually come
from an edible food source) sandwiched between two flavorless and off-color
buns. It was literally pressed onto my thin, Styrofoam tray with a handful of
french fries. They were still frozen. I loved that lunch lady. But I've always
brown-bagged it since then.

Flying

Kamaria Holden, age 13

In sixth grade, my homeroom teacher had just informed me that if I was late to homeroom one more time, she was going to give me two "U's" on my report card (a little harsh, don't ya think?). I didn't want that to happen. Since my second period teacher always let my class out late, I pledged to myself that I would run like the wind to homeroom everyday (crazy, I know).

The next day while I was running like a wild cheetah, this boy in my homeroom, who was about my height with black hair and brown eyes, thought, Hey, wouldn't it be hilarious to trip Kamaria? So, I was in my "cheetah zone" (nothing can stop me when I'm in my "cheetah zone") and, as I'm running, that boy slowly extends his leg and (now, you must imagine this part in slow motion) next thing I know, I'm in the air. My backpack goes soaring, and books fly all over the place.

While I am in the air, that Nelly Furtado song starts floating through my head. You know, the one that goes, "I'm like a bird, I only fly away." For those few moments, I feel, believe it or not, so good. Then, I feel my legs and arms scraping the ground until every bone feels broken. Everyone is cracking up. I am so embarrassed. But, at the same time, I am happy because I knew I had just flown to the ground.

The Worst Saturday

Kyrsten Sprewell, age 14

We had a twenty-minute break during a Saturday session of school, only enough time to get out of your seat for a moment, eat, use the restroom, but still not talk. I did not bring a lunch so I sat down and wrote in my journal instead.

It's like a prison for rule-breakers instead of criminals. That's how they're treating us today. It's crazy. We laugh when we tell our friends we have to go and we joke about why we have to go, but it's still the worst Saturday of our lives. We work on the assigned 40-page packet and take a break. I did not bring a lunch. Don't you even look at me when I'm hungry? I'm mad, can you tell?

By now, we are all ready to hurt the teachers who made us come today. We want them to feel our pain. Maybe I'm exaggerating, maybe I'm not, but it's still the worst Saturday ever.

NO TALKING, NO GUM, NO GETTING OUT OF YOUR SEAT, NO LAUGHING, NO CELL PHONES, NO BATHROOM, NO BLINKING, NO SHOWING YOUR TEETH, YOUR EYES, YOUR FACE, NO TO PRETTY MUCH ANYTHING.

I'm soooooooooooo bored. ZZZZZZZZZZZZZZZZZZZZZZZZZZ. BAM.

"Hello, Kyrsten, what world are you from? There is NO sleeping in Saturday School."

"What can I do, man?"

"Just for that, you'll have Saturday school for the next 3 weeks!!!"

Oh, no, here we go again!

When you love someone,
it's a great jumping off point for writing,

Write what you know
and what you don't know.

Labels

Alexandra Bonin, age 18

While writing this piece about my experience at school, I was able to positively express my thoughts and feelings through poetry.

I listen to them

I hear their words

words of disappointment,

feelings of inadequacy

feeling hopeless, like a little boat lost

in a great swirl of water, waiting,

just waiting, for the massive whirlpool

it's coming

it's coming

almost there.

I hear words of hate,

disgust

I see eyes, eyes of accusation and dislike

turn upon me.

I feel hot beads of sweat form at the back of my neck.

I feel like I am on display, like a circus freak —

"The Oblivious White Girl.

Please do not pelt with banana peels,

no matter how much you want to."

I feel like this label is plastered on me,

plastered on like some sort of Mark of Cain

a mark, vivid and bright, that can never come off,

no matter how hard I rub it.

They tell me they do not want to feel guilt.

But is it not natural for me to feel it?

What else can I offer them?

What else can I feel, to show them that I care,

That their struggle matters to me?

The damage has been done

I cannot escape the role I was born into,

as much as I might try.

I want to escape,

I want to understand,

I do not wish to remain oblivious and ignorant.

I want to apologize for the acts of my fathers

Why remain in the dark?

But how to get to the light?

Chapter 4 { Friendship }

True & Loyal, Fiercely So

Writer's Block (an excerpt)

Abby Anderson, mentor

I wrote this script, "Writer's Block," as a way to get over my own writer's block. Bob, an eccentric renowned screenwriter gives advice to his personal assistant, Devin, a recent film school grad.

INT. BOB'S STUDY - MORNING

The next morning, DEVIN enters the study. He's mid-20s, a skinny guy with a cheap student haircut. BOB, a white-haired, bearded man in his mid-60s, is at his desk, writing. Bob writes in longhand, in pencil, on a yellow legal pad. He's the kind of weird old man the neighborhood kids tell strange stories about.

Devin sees a script sitting on Bob's desk.

DEVIN
So, did you get a chance to read my script?

BOB
The first ten pages.

DEVIN
Oh, okay. I'll just leave it with you 'til you have time to read the whole thing. I'll be in the kitchen.

Devin heads out of the room.

BOB
I don't need to read the whole thing. I can tell by the first ten pages it's crap.

Devin turns in the doorway, totally shocked.

BOB (Cont'd)
Sit down.

Devin drops into a folding chair. Bob taps the script.

BOB
Devin, have you ever witnessed a plane crash?

DEVIN
No, not personally.

BOB
Known anyone who was in a plane crash?

DEVIN
I'm from Minnesota.

BOB
Did you do any research about plane crash survivors?

DEVIN
Well ... I watched Castaway a bunch of times and I read the book written by the guys from Alive. You, know, the Argentinean soccer team.

BOB
Have you ever been stranded anywhere or done any extreme wilderness survival training?

DEVIN
I was a Boy Scout. We went camping a bunch of times . . . but we had tents and stuff.

BOB
Have you ever even been on a plane?

DEVIN
Yeah, of course. How do you think I got out here to go to college?

BOB
And since then?

Devin shifts around in the hot seat.

DEVIN
I flew home for a visit once. I haven't really been able to afford to go home more than that one time.

BOB
So, of the three planes that you've been on, have any of them almost crashed?

DEVIN
No.
(a beat)
But there was some turbulence. I even spilled my drink.

In his desk chair, Bob wheels himself around to the far side of the desk.

BOB
In the Poetics, Aristotle identified six characteristics of the perfect story: plot, character, thought, language, spectacle and the writer's own experience. In other words, "write what you know."

DEVIN
That's crazy! "Write what you know?" If that were

really true, there'd be no science fiction, no historical stuff, no characters of the opposite sex, no animation –

He trails off, momentarily flustered. When he regains his composure, he looks at Bob.

DEVIN (Cont'd)
Have you ever fought in a war?

BOB
No.

DEVIN
But you won an Oscar for writing a war movie! According to you, it should only have been written by a veteran.

BOB
I didn't say "write what you know" applied to me. Only to you.

DEVIN
What?! Why?

BOB
'Cause you don't know what you're doing yet.

Devin doesn't have an answer to that.

The Belly Button Club

Wendy Tigerman, mentor

Established in 1956, The Belly Button Club was always an exclusive organization. Maximum membership, two: one inney and one outey. The mission, agenda and anthem of The Belly Button Club was uncontrollable laughter. Beyond the lame humor appealing to six year-olds, it was my cousin Karen's ridiculous size that transformed our clubhouse into a loony bin. I don't think she was legally a midget or anything, but, man, she was the tiniest, skinniest little thing. I pretty much look like a moon-faced hulk standing next to her in all the photographs. But long before cute boys showed up at her birthday parties, it was no big deal. Karen's diminutive stature caused her to slide out of chairs, slip between beds, and frequently fall through tight spaces. The descent cracked us up, but it wasn't until she got good and stuck that we went totally nutso. Karen managed to get lodged between our shoved-together fold-aways, barely deep sofa cushions, and even the front and rear seats of my mom's Studebaker. In winter when my parents removed the pads from their outdoor furniture, the redwood frames looked like a swell place for a Belly Button Club meeting. Who would have thought that Karen's puny butt could actually squeeze between the tight ropes of the patio chaise? But it took only one or two bounces for my best friend to become neatly folded between the taut twine. Karen was wedged so tightly, and we were so weakened by hysteria, that my dad had to be called to perform an emergency extraction. He wielded his upholstery sheers like the surgeon he had once hoped to be. Years later we told everyone he had used the jaws of death. By the time Karen and I were in our early twenties, we'd grown apart and the Belly Button Club had long been on hiatus. She was on the Hollywood fast- track to becoming a cinematographer with a brand new guild card in her pocketbook. I was living in a Tibetan Buddhist Meditation community just below timber line of the Colorado Rockies when I got the news. In her retro Fairfax apartment, Karen had put on an old Buffalo Springfield album, brewed some chamomile tea, and placed the thrift shop china cup by the side of her claw foot tub. Slipping into the steaming bath, she passed out, bashing her forehead on the faucet and sliding down beneath ten inches of water. The autopsy revealed high levels of cocaine in Karen's petite body and suggested she had suffered a heart attack. Family members still prefer to call it death by drowning. Cousin Karen was the sister I always wanted. The beautiful, delicate being I longed to be. Laughing from the gut remains my life anthem. And The Belly Button Club, reduced to a membership of one, the outey, remains an organization unspoiled by politics, fundraising, or taking itself too seriously.

This piece came from a writing experiment at the Fiction Workshop:
"Tell us about an imaginary friend you had when you were a kid."

Elecía

Stephanie Almendarez, age 18

Elecía lived in my 11-year-old imagination, tangled in the garden of my dreams. The first time I caught a glimpse of her was with my little brother. Elecía went everywhere I went, but she was not always physically present.

She was a tiny little thing you could confuse with a moth or butterfly. She was silent like the wind and loving as the sky. Her face was cute and small. She had a button nose and big eyes for a little girl. She was always there, warning me not to do bad things. She'd come up to scold me in my face, fluttering in her magenta aura. "Stephanie! Stephanie!" she'd say, "No!" Her mouth opened into a wide O, "Don't call him!"

Treehugger

Alexandra Bonin, age 18,

EXT. PARK - DAY

FROGURT, wearing a mischievous
expression and a cowboy hat,
hangs from a tree. Down below,
STANLEY, his best friend,
used to putting up with
Frogurt's theatrics, listens
while Frogurt reminisces.

FROGURT
In all my life, the most
embarrassing thing that ever
happened to me was . . . the
time I had to hug a tree.

Frogurt slips from the tree
a little. Stanley urges him
to maintain his grip.

STANLEY.
Keep on huggin' it!

Frogurt is upset.

FROGURT
How did you get me to do
this? And why do I continue
to do it?

STANLEY
Hug it good!

FROGURT
If you're trying to get me
to respect nature, this isn't
working.

Three PASSERSBYS spot Frogurt
up the tree and look disgusted
at the display.

PASSERBY #1
That's the sickest thing
I've ever seen!

FROGURT
No, wait! It's not what
you think!

PASSERBY #2
You know, if you wanted
to do that kind of thing,
you could've used a
houseplant, indoors!

PASSERBY #3
Wow, that's not cool.

FROGURT
Wait, no, I'm cool!
I've got pizzazz!

Passerby #3 taunts
Frogurt and Stanley.

PASSERBY #3
And a leopard-print
cowboy hat!

STANLEY
OK, Frogurt, you can
come down, now that you
admit that Telemundo is
a work of art.

FROGURT
How dare you sully my
good name by spreading
that slanderous filth.

Three days later . . .

Frogurt, still hugging
the tree, snickers down
at Stanley.

FROGURT
You know, Stanley, the word
"gullible" is not in the
dictionary.

Stanley thumbs through a
dictionary and then looks
blankly at Frogurt.

FROGURT (CONT'D)
What? It really isn't?

Frogurt looks down, straining
to see the dictionary. He
loses his grip and falls off
the tree. On the ground, he
rights himself and grabs the
dictionary, rifling through it
to see if the word is there.
Slowly, he looks over at
Stanley.

FROGURT
Touché.

Best Fiction tip:

You can never tell too
many lies in fiction.

What's Real (an excerpt)

Kimberly Minten Purcell, mentor

I gazed down the Santa Monica Promenade and saw Becky and two of her new
popular friends, Veronica Benson and Jody Smith, walking right toward me. I
had the worst luck. I considered ducking back into the shop, but they'd seen
me. The three of them were strutting, shoulders touching, like some six-armed,
six-legged monster. They were wearing pink shirts, all super tight. Becky had
even pierced her belly button like the other two. I wondered if her mom knew.
She gave her new best friends a look and they stopped three feet away. I felt this
horrible sense of dread.

"Hey, Meg." Her voice sounded nearly genuine, but not. She'd taken on the
undulating tone of the other girls, and her voice dipped and swayed too much
to be real. "Who're you here with?" She looked around as if I had a crowd of
friends lined up waiting to talk to me after she and her pals had dissed me to
everyone in the school.

I hesitated. Was it better to say my mom, or nobody? Both options sucked, but
it would be weird to be standing there if I wasn't waiting for anyone. "My mom."
Becky exchanged a look with Veronica. I stared at her, trying to figure out how
she could possibly be the same friend I'd had for the last five years.

"Did you hear Veronica's going to the dance with David?" I had heard they were
seeing each other.

"Yeah?" I said, bored, like I didn't care. They'll look ridiculous together, I told
myself. She was way too tall for him. Veronica tossed her long, dark hair back
in an arrogant gesture, an I-am-the-winner look, and I could see she knew all
about my five-year crush on David. I wanted to walk away, but I feared their

taunting laughter. Just one month ago, I'd been laughing with them at a dorky girl at school who spoke too loudly for their liking. I was no better than Becky, really. Maybe we could still be friends, even after everything that had happened.

"You going to be around for Christmas?" I asked her.

"Yeah, why?" She glanced at the others and seemed nervous.

"Maybe, um, maybe we could talk." My voice squealed at the end of my sentence, showing my pitiful weakness.

Veronica was looking at me like I had two heads. Becky caught her look and stated emphatically. "We already talked."

"No, we didn't," I said, but it came out weak, like I was begging. She was burying me in my grave, and I was grasping for her leg. Please, don't do it, I cried, and she shoveled in more dirt.

She gave me a look of pity. That was it. My best friend was gone.

Lily

Ashley Wilson, mentor

There are many ways to survive, and people who say there is only one way — hard labor where you earn your keep — by and large live off inherited money. Lily Esposito, a petite woman nearing forty, has survived (though at times it looked iffy) on wit and humility. She isn't a great beauty, but exudes attitude and charm. Her shiny brown hair curls randomly around a face that one moment seems enchanting only to become rather plain the next. Dark circles beneath her animated eyes tell of insomnia and strange eating habits. She's skilled, bright, and educated.

If you ask, she'll tell you that she's worked in advertising, modeling, publishing, PR and so on. She'll recreate a typical day in each profession, bringing hilarious co-workers to life, pointing out delicious ironies and revealing the fundamental futility of American capitalism. "It's true!" she'll shriek and bounce in her seat, and it might be. She's held many jobs, just never stayed long. Then again, she could be lying.

Mention the Los Angeles riots, New Orleans during Hurricane Katrina, the fall of the Berlin Wall; she's lived through them all. She has moved a lot, so she might have. She'll claim that she attended art school on scholarship in San Francisco, partied with starlets on Sunset Strip and drove a Volkswagen Bug spray-painted with the words "God is dead" through Alabama. Kansas, she'll swear, is a giant cornfield filled with signs warning of the Apocalypse; Florida has more Cadillacs than Cubans; and the cockroaches in Texas are the size of tangerines. She'll defend these statements to her last breath.

Lily married at nineteen and divorced at twenty-nine. A few years later, she moved in with a fiancé, left him and met her current husband. Each of these men had money. I am not saying Lily uses men; she's not strategic. She has a true and loyal heart, fiercely so. She has slept with a great many men, rich and poor. Perhaps only the wealthy ones stuck around.

Last April, I visited her growing family in Atlanta. Her kind, British husband is thriving as a top manager in an insurance company. They're more in love than ever. She has a perfectly behaved five-month-old. She has lost all the baby weight. She goes religiously to a gym. Her hair, still without a single grey, isn't dyed. Her current writer's salon has more published writers and greater talent than the ones she started in New York, San Fran or L.A. But then, she could be lying.

Life

Maia Akiva, mentor

This scene is about a relationship with a friend who seems to be happier than me. It's a philosophical piece about how to live life, how to be happy.

INT. ROOM - ANYTIME

A woman and a man, MEL and NATHAN, sit on opposite sides of a room. Nathan sits on a chair; Mel sits on the floor. Mel is sad and lifeless; Nathan is happy and full of life. After a moment, Nathan turns around. He notices Mel. He stands up and walks over to her.

NATHAN
Hi.

MEL
Hi.

NATHAN
I've been in here for a while, but I only just now noticed you.

MEL
I've been here for a while, too, and I've never seen you before.

NATHAN
I'm Nathan.

MEL
Mel.

A beat.

NATHAN
So, how long have you been in this room?

MEL
Thirty-one years. You?

NATHAN
Thirty-five years. Do you like it in here?

Mel looks around and shrugs.

MEL
It's a tough room.

NATHAN
It's a room. The rest is what you make of it.

MEL
Do you like it?

Nathan walks around, touching the walls.

NATHAN
I wouldn't want to be anywhere else.

MEL
Why? What's so great about this place? Look at it. It's just walls with nothing inside. It sucks.

NATHAN
No. Look at all of the space and the four corners. Each corner is different from the others. It's so interesting.

MEL
They all look the same to me.

She walks over to one corner.

MEL (CONT'D)
This one is a corner.

She moves to another corner.

MEL (CONT'D)
And this is another corner —
exactly the same as the other
one. This room is so empty.
No matter what I do, I just
end up in a corner. This
room's a bitch and then
you die.

NATHAN
Well, I'm sorry you feel that
way. I get sad and frustrated
here sometimes, but it's part
of being here.

Nathan starts singing a song.
Mel looks at him, aggravated.

MEL
What are you so happy about?

NATHAN
Me. You. This room. Everything. What are you so upset
about?

MEL
Me. You. This room.

NATHAN
Why? You're here. You're
healthy.

MEL
It's not that simple.

NATHAN
I know it's not simple.
But it's great. Look at it.
This room is great. We're
having a conversation. We
both can sit down if we
want to. Or we can stand
up if we want to.

MEL
What do you know about
what I'm going through?
You have a chair! You
don't have to sit on the
floor all the time. And eat
on the floor. And worry all
the time about not having
a chair.

The T-Shirt

AJ Reza, age 14

The t-shirt was pink and purple with a bright pink palm tree and the word "cool" plastered across the front. I had no idea where it came from. According to my mother, it was a hand-me-down from my best friend Lauren. Maybe that's why I kept it for so long. For me, it was a symbol of a friendship that lasted forever and then unceremoniously fell apart.

I saw Lauren a few years ago at summer camp. I wore the shirt and asked if she remembered it. She said no. That hurt somehow. I know it was just a shirt, nothing more. But I felt like Lauren was saying no so nonchalantly about me, too. Like she could forget all about me.

Soon after, we lost contact and my mom threw the shirt away.

Write a letter to a friend,

then burn it

or mail it.

Goofy, serious, fun and annoying: friends can be rich sources of inspiration.

Chapter 5 {Coming Of Age}

The Stress of the Present

Write something

you wish you could do, or would have done.

Write about change — that is really what a good story is all about.

Vent about your past.
Very therapeutic.

In Defense of Nostalgia

Ariel Edwards-Levy, age 16

I've noticed recently that most of my writing tends to deal with the past. This piece was an attempt to justify that tendency and explain it to myself.

I've been told, on occasion, that I live too much in the past. There's probably some merit to the claim, but there's also some merit to the predictable comforts of days already passed and stories already told, like old children's movies re-watched so often that the pictures get jumpy in places and the dialogue is so familiar that it goes unheard. Watching those movies, I never remember the plot, but I remember where I saw them for the first time and with whom.

It's the same nostalgia that keeps my middle school orchestra CDs stacked by my computer. Sometimes the stress of the present disconnects me so much from the past that it seems as if my childhood was another old movie: familiar, yet fictitious, starring someone else. But one note of violin solo, and suddenly I'm fidgeting on our creaky old stage, the air gritty from rosin dust and warm from stage lights and a lack of air-conditioning. I react viscerally to bowstrings and downbeats. As the sound swells, I am graduating, feeling shell shocked, regretful, and proud as I walk across the stage. The music hits a minor key — sad, but not bitter — the failed tests, the missed opportunities, the lost friendships. The music ends, the curtain falls, and I'm plunged screaming back into junior year. I need to immerse myself in the past, or I will simply divorce myself from it, look at that girl who is supposed to be me, and cite irreconcilable differences.

Before

Jennifer Carcamo, age 16

Before today, I was millions of things. I was thirteen before. I was seven before. I was even one little year old, if you can believe that. I was considered a hillbilly before. I was Nikita's best friend. I was also Marla's, Diana's, Lizbeth's, Kathleen's, Melissa's, Valerie's, Nicky's, Cameron's, Farisha's, Tiffany's, and Monica's best friend before. I used to like Tonio, Manuel, Justin, Ronald, and Roger as more than friends before. I was looked up to for my perkiness before. I was the most popular girl in elementary school before. I was the best artist before. I was the fastest runner before. I watched and saw things that I now think are stupid before. I have seen policemen's cars park in front of my house and take away the least expected.

I have seen my grandparents, parents, uncles, aunts, little cousins and all of the people I know cry before. I have danced like crazy before. I have swum in the open sea and in the depths of the coldest lakes, before. I've been to California, Missouri, Arkansas, Oklahoma, Arizona, Nevada, Alabama, New Mexico, Tennessee, Texas, Kansas, Mexico, and even El Salvador before! I have flown in a plane, tasted sushi, fallen and made deep scars, run a mile, thrown a disc, lost over two hundred dollars, sung the weirdest song, given an oral presentation, broken a cup, fixed something, said something nasty, said something that would make one think, written an essay before. And much more. I was all of the above before today, and before many other todays. Now, my eyes scan the top of this document and reread what I have been before. And now I scan the bottom of the page and find white space waiting to be filled through the eyes of before.

P.S. Whoever stole my $200, I want it back.

A Tax on Salt

Marlys West, mentor

Reading about the furor over James Frey's autobiography and talking to Lena, my mentee, about the outrage some people felt made me think about my own little foray into autobiographical prose poetry. Our conversation reminded me that something true isn't always something factual, maybe especially so in creative writing.

I swallow the river and the fish swim into me. You know that feeling of being deeply, gladly alive? Right now, I don't have it. Gandhi bade his followers to come with him to the sea and make their own salt boiling warm, ocean water. My grandmother's last sister died two years ago. I should have kept in touch. I should have written. Now they're all nine dead. Gus and Woodrow, Ruth and Una, the others. Even my grandmother's missing, her ashes scattered over water and the water gone to its maker, the Gulf. I hope I've drunk her. I hope I've swum through her like I swam through my father and mother. Once when my Uncle Woody drove me downtown, we crossed four lanes of highway to get to his exit. We were practically perpendicular to oncoming traffic in an old, green pick up truck. This was Highway 10 and no one touched us. I wasn't wearing a seatbelt. If that happened today, I'd be dead. He was old when I was a girl. Now I'm a woman and have made my own mistakes. I should have invited everyone to the wedding, but I didn't and have lived to regret it. That and the rest of my misdeeds. Sometimes my grandmother rattles through the pipes and drains. I should have listened to what her little ghost voice said and invited everyone. Should not have tripped my youngest brother that one time he left the table carrying his plate. Sure, right, I was young, but still I wince just thinking of his poor, startled face. In the old days the colonists were mad about the tax on tea. I read all about it. Boxes of black leaves dumped into the ocean. In my family most people like coffee. But there are some who prefer herbal tea. My freckles have come out this summer, and I'm glad I have so much to write about — like the time I killed the next-door flowers using dog food dust, bleach and salt. It was an experiment. I didn't think I'd knock out an entire garden, but I did. Luckily no one found out, but I remember the flowers died standing on their stalks, and I could see them from my bedroom window, a mess of husks and brown carcasses. It put something sharp in my gut — a hot, guilty star. Even now I can smell the bleach and salt and horsemeat concoction I carried across the street in a large, open-mouthed jar.

My Secret Life as an Aging Emo Fan

Hilary Galanoy, mentor

Ooof. My back hurt by the end of the evening, and I got home past 1 a.m. — late for what I still refer to as a "school night," even at age 37. The cause of my exhaustion? Getting down at The Fall Out Boy concert – backstage, no less! I've been to a number of emo rock shows in the last few months: FOB, The Academy Is, and Panic! At the Disco (twice).

Now, if you're over 25, you probably have never heard of these bands. I know I certainly hadn't. These bands aren't meant to be liked, admired, or followed by "adults." It's music made by youth for youth. Like every generation — my parents with the Beatles, me with Duran Duran — we have our own music that we grow up to and identify with as tortured and talented and rebellious and that makes us dream of being rock stars ourselves, or at least dating one.

I thought I was beyond the live music, concert-going phase of my life (unless it was an "oldies" tour of 1980's one-hit wonders, or jazz). But I'm friends with a music agent who is always offering to take me along to these hip concerts. I work from home, so I like to get out and socialize at night. Why not? At first, I figured it would be more enjoyable if I downloaded songs to familiarize myself with this new "emo" style — maybe even learn a few lyrics. And then somewhere along the way, I actually grew to like the music. FOB's "From Under the Cork Tree" is getting more play nowadays on my iPod than my usual "adult contemporary" stand-bys of Coldplay and U2. And suddenly I found I was rocking-out, singing along. I was probably one of the oldest fans in the stadium — except for the parents who drove their kids. (Although I might be older than some of them, as well.) I'd feel like a groupie except that maturity has taught me to wear sensible shoes and make sure to eat dinner beforehand so the heat and the crowds don't make me feel faint.

As I nursed my beer at the surprisingly tame after-party, I couldn't help but smile at the fact that most of the boys in these punk bands aren't even old enough to legally drink. Ah, youth. But I can't help wonder if being part of this music scene is a way for me to hold onto my own. As lyricist Pete Wentz from Fall Out Boy writes, "Dance, dance, we're falling apart to half-time. Dance, dance — and these are the lives you'd love to lead…"

Wisdom

Ashtynn Baltimore, age 14

Wisdom is rich with butter,

Fat with carbs

And healthy with flavor.

Good for the soul,

Only nourished with experience.

The Age Of Certainty

Allison Deegan, mentor

In times like these, surrounded by people who know better, my nerve wavers.

I am supposed to know since no one else does where you are going, yet they talk and talk. I am not certain of the promises I make, the happiness I predict, but I say these things in earnest.

I want everything to be true, secure, since that would only be fair, but I also know that fair is elusive.

Doing the best I can, thinking with my heart, advising without guile, are not formidable enough for the responsibility I have to you.

There is no wizened author's manual, explaining how to get it right the first time, the only time, what may be the very last time we have.

I am left to look where I always look, reading the trees, going inside, casting off the things nature has no time for, instinct over media in the end.

This is why others turn to scriptures, follow prophets, the need to know being so intoxicating, so nagging it clouds the brain and chases sleep.

But I understand that gilt edges and thrones and pronouncements of infallibility are not the same as being sure, and I am not sure because nobody is.

You will never blame me for what I did not know, and that makes it harder still.

I will know, the Santa Ana winds will know, and I am certain I will document my failings at some point in the future, finally writing that book, certain you will read it.

Death, Love, Growth, Hatred

Mara Bochenek, age 17

Most things are inevitable: death, love, growth,
Even hatred. Everyone does it.
Most people don't like to admit it, but I do.
And for the first time I'm not sad about it.

Everyone goes through death. I've been through three,
Two that I can remember, and another one on the way.
Love is something that can't be categorized.
I don't really know what it is, when it happened or even if I'm in it now.

Growth is something I do every day.
I learn something new, and with that comes change.
But there is another experience that people don't like to talk about
It's hate, and it's a very strong word.

Hate is the only word that fully describes how someone feels toward another.
There are many levels of hate. There's the "I'm just laying around."
And there's "I love you — hate you," or the hatred of "they,"
Where you just flat out want to punch someone in the face every time you see him.

Hate is a very strong word, but it has many meanings
That everyone everywhere feels.
Out of death, love, growth or hatred, hatred is the one thing that everyone
Will go through in their lifetimes.

They could live lives without the loss of someone they care about.
They could never know what love is, and they could never do anything new to grow.
Hate is the one thing that everyone has in common.
It's the one thing everyone feels.

Thin as a Wafer

AJ Reza, age 14

Thin as a wafer

But alive as a telephone wire

Always the first to

Lead in a belching contest

They were my communion

My daily bread.

Life seemed to be ours

In these moments

The fast breaks

In a rusty wire

My world, or at least

Parts of it.

Even if only for a summer

Or a few

Like slippers

Quick on, quick off

Or at least until your

Feet are warm.

Where Do They All Go?

Karly Abreu, age 15

The water droplets make fish eyes in the shower drain.

Where do they all go?

The girls in the swimming pool are mermaids in chlorine.

Where do they all go?

Angels are transparent blue, with smiling faces, and wispy beards.

Where do they all go?

The rainbow is no longer a magical blessing, a sign of God's love.

It's the reflection of sunlight on the mist.

How can this be?

Sunrise is no deep mystery, nor the spinning of the stars.

We are too old to believe in such nonsense.

We must trade our fantasy for fact.

But I still wonder —

Faeries once sat out in the snow.

Where do they all go?

Childhood

Melina Zúniga, age 15

Ever wish things were back to the way they used to be?

Back when eight o'clock was late

When saying sorry meant we're friends again

When a hug fixed everything

When you couldn't stay angry for more than an hour

When things weren't so complicated

And when playtime never seemed to end?

Those were the times to savor

When did our childhoods end?

Abstract

Paloma Elsesser, age 14

When I was a child
everyone's eyes followed me

I looked in the mirror
judging myself
I wanted to venture
to the wise stars over me
dance on my questions that make me live again

The closed doors around me
gave me inner secrecy and security
My vague dreams lifted out of the ground
the shapes in my mind rising up
floating above the craziness

The walls with all their bland, solemn imagery
were rough,
Pretty objects got old for me
A girl gets sick of a rose

The flickers of dishonesty were silver and exact
My immature ponderings
could be compared to lilacs that seem to die

But in my mind
It was all insane
My mind was the hurrying of tumbling waves
and quick broken crests
My life was abstract

Chapter 6 { Women }

born a girl born a girl born a girl born a girl born a girl born a girl born a girl born a girl born a girl born a girl born a girl born a girl born a girl born a girl born a girl born a girl born a girl born a girl born a girl born a girl

Born A Girl

I write because...

I write because there is nothing else to do when I am sitting at home and the television bores me and plucking my brows bores me and my husband is busy and the baby is napping and the only thing I have is myself and my thoughts and they're never boring.

Saccharine

Ariel Edwards-Levy, age 16

There's a certain kind of woman, sweet and disingenuous, who's like nothing so much as artificial sugar. In Los Angeles, she's nearly ubiquitous; walk into any restaurant, and you'll see a dozen girls modeled after her, blissfully wrapped in pastel colors and good marketing. Walk by, and she'll flash you a maraschino smile, teeth bleached to an Aspartame white. She's all chemical, all refinement and blue food coloring #1, saccharine, mawkish, and a little poisonous. Sit next to her, and you'll start to feel a little self-conscious. How could you not? She's "great taste without all the calories." She isn't real. And the truth is that real life and real sugar aren't as sweet.

Real life is messy, and it rarely comes in pretty packaging. It isn't pure. It doesn't sparkle, and sometimes, you get fat. It's never glamorous to be the plain brown package, overlooked at the back of the coffee shop. And so, maybe it's she who's taken the path of least resistance by staying perfect, pristine — from her frosted hair to her phony coloring — until the day when the side effects begin to show.

Young Geography

Lena Brooks, age 17

I wrote this poem while reading "Nantucket," by Herman Melville. It's about adolescence but I don't think I learned any more about adolescence.

In the interest of becoming a woman
I became Stonecreek, Alabama.
My name was dueling banjoes and I reeked of sea.
I woke in the morning and vomited
tangerines until I was full of nothing,
braided my long hair until I looked
like a fish and was a fragrant drunk.
I flew up the banks of mother time.
I looked up her skirt, I crashed into her thighs.
Saw immense salt water mastadon
mammals born of mother time,
lost all idea of gender and floated down
sexless ashes, black soot. Arrested flesh
until I was defined and kept a journal
on my skin: Exist only in rhyme, pentameter,
cotton-picking minutes. Live hymnally!
Threw myself quietly at scripture teachers
and the splitters open of self. And came to
adolescence in the arms of psychedelic experience.
Was first kissed by beat and stayed up
late at night to read good words, think hot thoughts,
be only short breaths between bed sheets.

Just Keep Them Waiting

Karen Girard, mentor

At the Fiction Workshop, we were asked to describe a family member using all five senses. I had just returned from visiting my 97-year-old grandmother. She thought I'd be a great writer but a terrible cook, and kept trying to teach me cooking basics. One day, long after I'd mastered all her cooking secrets, she realized it didn't matter whether I could cook at all. I had choices she never had.

Nana shuffles across the green linoleum,

puts a dented aluminum pot from the '30s

on a goldenrod stove from the '70s.

As dinner sizzles in the pan,

she cups spices in her gnarled velvet hand.

Look, she says, this is a teaspoon,

and sprinkles a few more

grains of fragrant dust,

that's a tablespoon.

You've got to know this,

to cook for a husband someday.

Her white feather curls tremble as she glances

over her scarlet-sweatered shoulder.

You want to cook for a husband

once you're out of college, don't you?

Cornered, I kiss her powder-white cheek,

say nothing. What can I say

that I haven't said before?

She laughs, blue eyes sparkling,

like lightning out of a clear sky.

Oh, you're too dumb to get caught

by the men just yet, aren't you, honey?

As crispy, perfect pork chops

slide onto our plates, she advises,

just keep them waiting.

They can fix their own damn dinner.

For Barbie

Lovely Umayam, age 18

Birds of paradise shrivel before your
red painted cheeks and
magenta blotched lips,
forty-inch nails primed like knives,
used for catfights
that you never won.

Minutes of prodding,
plastering lids with
superficial ink tips,
spitting immaculate litanies out of
your thorny throat that echo hollow in
eavesdropping bathroom stalls.

Poking brave eyes with
utensils of death,
battering lashes
with supercilious struts,
vanity entombed forever.

I enjoy reading poems about work, but never see enough poems about women's work.

Bridal Registry

Cece Peri, mentor

We work our way
down the aisles, down the list
picked thin by the bride's
family and friends.
My daughter and I
left with little else
but serving spoons & ladles
the backbones of domesticity.

Another glance at the list reveals
an overlooked item: heated towel rack.

I gather up my weary grandson
as my daughter takes the item
to the register
to be removed from the list, and wrapped

Later,
she, who not so long ago
was herself a bride who believed
in warm towels,
folds the list and lets it slip
into a wastebasket.

"Soon," she says, "they'll see,
they won't need half those things."

And there, in the Bed and Bath Department of Macy's,
I want to put my arm around her,
or at least run my hand
over those errant strands
of auburn hair.
Instead, I shift
the sleeping boy on my hip.

women

123

What Is Beauty All About?

Kyrsten Sprewell, age 14

One night, I was working with my mentor, Amy Morton, and we couldn't find anything to write about. I asked her to give me a first line. She gave me this: "She started to think as she stood in front of the sink."

She started to think as she stood in front of the sink
What is beauty all about, is beauty on the inside or out?

They say I'm not good enough; I'm not up to par
My mom says I'm up to ten on the beauty bar

But if 100 people say I'm not good enough, then it must be true
Nobody believes in me except for you

The mirror, it's said, tells the truth
But rating yourself is very uncouth

Is my life too much about my looks?
My grandmother says I should be reading some books

I guess I'm not going to be to everyone's taste
I guess people will always hate

But in the end I hope I will make it
And being put down, I'll just have to take it

Why?

Shawna Herron, age 17

Please leave me alone

Give me my privacy

Let me be me

Because I'm tired of being molded

Into somebody I'm clearly not

Stop telling me

That I am a girl

And therefore should act it

I may be a girl

But I am an individual

Who's not going to become

A housewife just because

I was born a girl.

Be happy

That I'm not going to give myself

To a man who's not my husband

Stop trying to make me wear clothes

That emphasize my curves

For a man's viewing pleasure

I may be a girl

But I'm still an individual

Don't tell me what to be

Just because

I was born a girl.

Daughter

Kate Gale, mentor

Learn how to fight. Learn how to fight back. Don't let anyone hit you. Don't let anyone hurt you. Learn how to get away. Learn how to get away quickly. Learn how to leave in the middle of the night. Learn how to leave while he is sleeping. Learn how to take care of yourself. Learn how to take care of your children. Learn how to take care of your brother. Learn how to run. Learn how to look over your shoulder. Learn how to run in the dark. Learn how to swim. Learn how to ride a wild horse. Learn how to sail. Learn how to sail away. Learn how to make your own money. Learn how to save your own money. You will be careful. You will remember all I told you, won't you?

Intelligent female writers will
one day rule the earth.

Editing is like combing your hair. You don't leave the tangles in.
Or the burrs. Or whatever.

Chapter 7 { On Society }

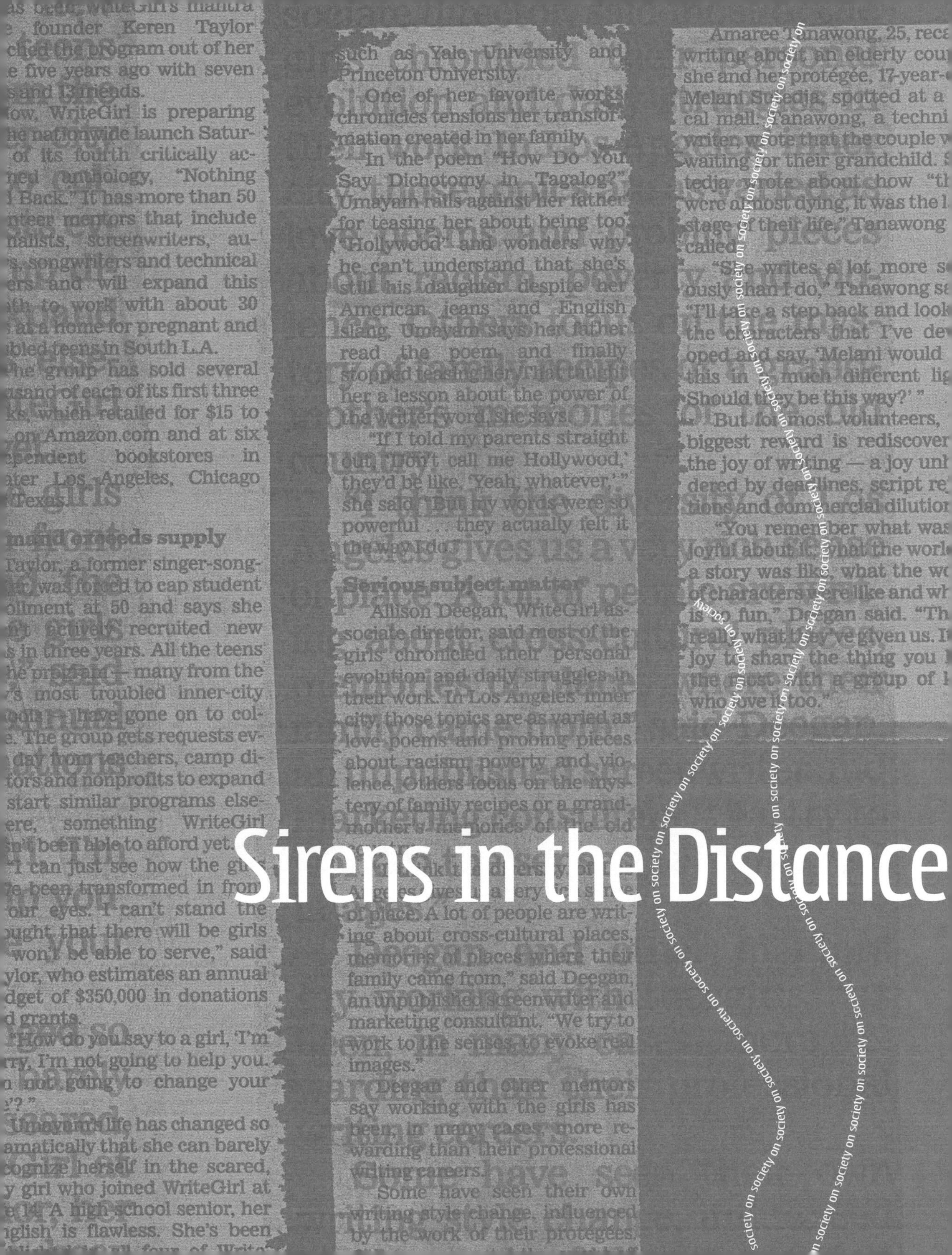

Sirens in the Distance

FICTION TIP :

WRITE FIRST WORRY LATER

Eyes of an Immigrant

Liliana Mendoza, age 17

This piece was inspired by the current immigration debate in Congress. A lot of people who are immigrants now or were before must have felt in some way like the character in my poem.

Going to a place where you've never been before
Trying to succeed at something, but they won't let you
School is out of the question
All that is left to do is work

They judge you by color or by sex
The pay is not enough
No money to buy food
No money to pay the rent
Kids are growing and growing hungrier
The little food you have all goes to them
But being skinny as a stick won't stop you
You want to see your kids succeed in life
Do things you couldn't do
Being able to say Hispanics do succeed
No matter how long it takes
You'll do what it takes

Being and Believing is who you are
But it won't help you in this state of mind
Where the put-downs and the breakdowns
Are all you can think of,
Telling yourself you don't belong here
But telling your kids you're here to stay
You think of the future
Thinking how great it would be then
Seeing your kids grow up and
Being able to say, "Look at me now, at all
I've achieved. I'm greater than ever."

A Beautiful Day in the Neighborhood

T. Faye Griffin, mentor

Saturday mornings my neighborhood takes on a Mr. Rogers-esque kind of quality. Located in the heart of Los Angeles, thus the name "Mid City," my neighborhood is bordered by Pico Boulevard to the south. On weekdays, Pico serves as a thoroughfare for Eastenders moving west on the Big Blue Bus toward Santa Monica to clean houses and to nanny babies. Westsiders, in turn, make their daily pilgrimage east towards Downtown in their Beemers and Benzes so they can afford to pay those who clean their houses and nanny their babies.

This particular Saturday morning, it's another beautiful day in the neighborhood. Birds sing. Lawns are watered. Little black kids skip past graffiti-riddled auto body shops to buy street treats at the Korean-owned liquor store. Large Latino families load and unload laundry in the crowded parking lot of Lucy's Fluff and Fold. And white folks in Nike gear who've recently moved into the newly gentrified pockets of the neighborhood jog without a care. All is right with the world except for the body of a young black man sprawled out at the bus stop on the southwest corner of Pico and Hauser.

As a rule, on Saturday mornings our stretch of Pico becomes an urban oasis where the fastest thing moving is usually Mr. Saunders from Dunsmuir Avenue walking his decrepit pooch. The dog is an ancient (but scrappy) little mongrel who no longer barks, but sort of coughs at you. He and his equally-as-old owner are the pace cars of the neighborhood. But on this day, the usually sparse and free-flowing Saturday traffic piles up as it tiptoes past the scene. It must have happened only moments before I tooled by. The authorities have not even arrived yet, though I hear the familiar blare of sirens in the distance.

With no yellow tape or body bags to prevent them from getting a good look, pedestrians and drivers alike take their time rubbernecking. Some cringe and turn away. Others openly gape, while still others calmly survey the scene to verify that it is not anyone they know.

I'm blessed with the knowledge that the young black man whose life force is spilling into a storm drain is neither Jonathan nor V.J. My sons are safely at home. So I drive on, having allowed my eyes to rest on the fallen young man for only a second. It is my lame attempt at giving him his dignity. My heart aches. This is some mother's child. My heart aches, and I cry on this beautiful day in the neighborhood.

Street Corner

Meghan McCarthy, mentor

My mentee, Gaby, had been working on a series of poems inspired by quotes from other pieces of literature. This was inspired by the quote, "I can only conclude that I am paying off karma at an increased rate."

I have no change

I tell him

Which is a lie

I am just in a hurry

And don't have time

To realize that

I am not better

just luckier

Averting Death by Boredom at the Conference

Geraldine Farrell, mentor

She'd pick the words, taste 'em a bit
or fancy 'em up with found meaning.
Either way she was certain they'd fit
into her careless collection, teaming
with terms, catch phrases or a sound lifted —
from the keynote's pontification
to a hushed utterance that drifted
through the white crowd for clarification.
On her list, today's favorites being:
"necrotization" and "comorbidity,"
juicy the jargon of rot and healing,
pathologies discussed with dexterity.
Grim words of concern physicians employ
now forever hers to abuse or enjoy.

This is an excerpt from a play about political campaign advisors. It was inspired by the news.

Campaign Trail

Allison Deegan, mentor

I ran a Senate campaign in Oklahoma in 1994. Burned a lot of bridges in the primary and had a tough opponent for the general election. Law and order, churchgoer, you know the type, clean on the outside, probably festering on the inside, heart attack waiting on deck if the Lord don't strike him down first. And us, running on brains and experience for a change, as if voters cared.

Then something incredible happened. My candidate, the man with whom I'd cast my lot, killed a panda bear. I'm not talking about Teddy, Smokey, Yogi or any bear you can think of, stuffed, cartoon or otherwise. I'm talking about a living, alive, panda bear, all the way from China. You like pandas? Of course you do. Everybody does. They are without a doubt the most beloved creatures on the face of the earth.

One sunny day on the campaign trail, my candidate, in a burst of civic pride and photo opportunity fever, drove around the grounds of the Oklahoma City Zoo on the new federally funded sidewalk sweeper. He jumps in the cockpit or whatever the heck they got on those things and starts it up. He's sweeping and waving to the press, having the time of his life, when he loses control of the damn thing and plows right into the new panda pavilion.

He nicks one of 'em, WaWa I think he's called, on the paw. Then he spins the wheel in a panic and ends up running smack into HeeHaw, or whatever the hell his name is, the male, squashing him flatter than a newspaper. Black and white and red all over, you see what I'm talking about? Dead panda, live at 5.

Kids are crying, the zoo manager is crying, even some of the reporters shed a tear. How do you recover from that? You don't. There is no constituency in the electorate that will say, "Killed a panda? We really don't care." They care.

But I was running the campaign that day. Was the candidate an idiot, run amok in a public facility, responsible for killing a beloved symbol of international friendship? No, he was a victim, and a hero, all rolled into one. That sweeper, see, was not manufactured in the great state of Oklahoma, and it had a small flaw. I didn't know what it was but I was sure a team of experts could find it. Something managed to override the candidate's careful piloting and the machine developed a crazed, dangerous mind all its own. Steering into that panda, wrangling control the best he could, he likely saved the lives of untold numbers of innocent little schoolchildren, perhaps the very ones who contributed pennies so the zoo could build that panda pavilion.

The zoo sued the manufacturer. The candidate sued. He was sporting one of those neck braces for quite some time — right through election day, as a matter of fact — an election he won once our opponent had the misfortune to question the official 'hero saves schoolchildren' story.

The man had panda bear blood on his hands and he was swept right into office, no pun intended. That, my boy, is politics. You understand what I'm saying? That's the league you're playing in now, the dead panda league. This ain't the student council, you know? Whatever dirt you're trying to smear around here, you can forget it. You can't scare me so don't even try.

Waiting. Waiting. Waiting.

Erica Kelly, mentor

There is only one working elevator for a six-floor building. Students come and go
throughout the day. The first class starts at 8 a.m. and the last ends at 10 p.m. It would
be worthwhile to invest in more elevators. But no. So I wait with twenty other students,
all with their bulging laptop cases, some with luggage that would not fit into an overhead
bin. All of them hoping to push their way onto the elevator, but knowing that not all of
them can. It finally comes, slowly opening and inviting the masses to squeeze in. They
look at me wondering if I, too, am going to climb aboard. But I look and wait. I'll just take
the next one.

Minutes pass and the elevator opens again. Luckily, only a few have traveled up from the
basement with their sodas and coffee in hand. I heave my bag onto my broad shoulder,
step onto the platform, and wait as the elevator stops for all the people. I'm always
waiting, wondering if they are ever going to get to my level.

Forces

Keren Taylor, mentor

Somehow, now, in war
clichés spring like geysers
"refrigerator words" as my poetry teacher called them
like ethical and responsibility
get in my way.
I very nearly used the word soul
trying to make sense, find meaning.
Even the shunned collective us or we
forces itself on me.
We go to the store, eat, sleep,
work, read the newspaper, have a glass
of Pinot Noir
while heads roll
tongues are cut out
limbs amputated.
Mothers break into pieces
into break Mother
pieces break into
bodies nailed in wooden boxes
in mail box
50,000 American soldiers with PTSD
depression, detachment,
estrangement,
17,649 wounded
2,349 killed
as of April 7, 2006
not including contractors, journalists,
soldiers from other countries or any Iraqis.
We are not counting them.
It is understood that the above list
may be incomplete.

Coffee or Tea?

Melissa Castillo, age 15

As I walk down the street I see them

In their wrinkle-free suits all fixed up

Hair straight back, walking step by step like robots

Cocky smile and smelling of thick ignorance

With their suitcases of hidden lies

They walk, catch cabs

Throw their cigarettes on the ground

Excellent day for them, they get out, pay the cab and into their offices they go

In their head they think, "Coffee or tea?"

Down the street one angel starves to death

Five blocks up a soul stops trying to fight and floats away

In the same building someone decides they've had enough

Across the street a girl's innocence was taken

And angels begin to cry

Coffee or tea?

Tookie

Angela Martinez, age 18

Today, after midnight, the newscaster said they were going to kill Tookie Williams with two poison shots. This is a situation that should be remembered.

I don't know much about this man, but when I saw on TV what he had done to those innocent people, I felt a cold chill through my body. I felt a bit sick. But I've been looking at all the people on TV praying and meditating. Maybe life should be taken away from him. Then again, doesn't everyone deserve a second chance? His case has been delayed for many years. Why now, after so long, does he get the penalty of death by lethal injection? Maybe this man learned his lesson. Maybe he changed. Is it right to kill somebody? Is there really justice?

This poem is about bulimia and, more subtly, about how people talk too much.

Execrable

Lilah Khoja, age 15

this is what we call w(retch)ed;

when words char your throat

with their dis(taste)ful meanings.

Speak up!

This is no time to be shy.

What am I scared of knowing?
What am I scared of thinking?

Concerto for Helicopter and Strings: A Love Song to Summer in Los Angeles (an excerpt)

Ariel Edwards-Levy, age 16

This is an excerpt from a much longer piece in which I attempted to document my last summer through a combination of anecdotes and generalities. It is also a work in progress. After nearly half a year, I'm still touching it up.

So if you want to sing along, please don't;
Welcome to the city, kid, and the summer of our discontent.
The heatstroked pavement is soaking all the color
out of monochrome swimming pools and half-hearted resolutions,
And the sun is an industrial stain on our wayward sky.

When I asked you where you'd been, you said up on the hill, watching the sun rise. It made me a bit jealous, because that's the sort of thing that constitutes an Experience, and I keep vowing to have one someday. But then I wasn't quite sure which I was jealous of, you or the sunrise, so I kept my mouth shut and went to breakfast

When Time Magazine had an article about being 13
I refused to read it.
I didn't want to find out how I had changed.
I didn't want to find out if I had changed at all.

But this isn't symbolic. We're at a concert, and so, when the blades raze over the melody, it's almost fitting, and didactic: "This is life," it says, "and these are interruptions, and who is to say which is the more beautiful?" You ponder this question in your band shirts and your ripped jeans, and you say,

"The rotors are staccato, in the key of E minor, but the musician wants to go home, and who can say which is which?" And of course you're right, you and your pretensions, relishing every sig alert and traffic jam. You lose your car keys and misplace your modifiers, and you almost killed your goldfish when you forgot to feed it for a week. You don't believe in politics, poetry, or Starbucks coffee.

Now is the summer of your discontent;
recycled themes and stolen lines,
three dollar gas and the unbearable brightness of being.
The moving finger writes, and, having writ,
Stands up and plays, a chance theory concerto,
A city sonatina.
The piano keys stick, and someone was smacking their gum.
The helicopter was the least of it.

Chapter 8 {Travel}

Speak through Gestures

Don't wait

for the perfect time or place or situation, just start writing — everywhere and anywhere.

I love letting my mind take me to another world on the page.

My mentor, Susan, and I each wrote poems about a trip we had taken, starting with "I remember." This is about a trip to Panama to visit my family.

Panama

Cydney Neal, age 13

I remember the skies and mountains that welcomed me into their home.

The different tropical colors of the clothing people wore.

Tropical jungles and inactive volcanoes.

Molas that everyone knew about.

Friendly locals who offered you everything.

Party buses that partied all night but worked all day.

Taxi cars without licenses.

The three-store malls.

The five-dollar jeans.

The Spanish you must know to get around.

All the appreciative people.

Gannets, watermelon.

The plantains, rice and fish.

The hand-made dresses that all the women had.

The skies and mountains that welcomed me into their home.

I learned that every trip has at least one good story, however embarrassing, and, as a writer, to push beyond conventional metaphors.

Sixteen-Euro Bellini

Maria Elena Rodriguez, mentor

My sister and I had planned a "budget" trip to Italy, just a few steps above the one I had taken as a poor exchange student twenty years ago. We knew prices were higher than in the States, but the dollar's daily slide against the Euro hit us like sticker shock. It now stood at a dismal $.72 to the Euro.

I'd booked us into an eighty-euro per night hotel in Mestre, a middle-class town just outside of Venice. It was still low season, but even one-star and no-star double rooms in Venice proper were over 200 Euros per night. A one-euro bus ride from Mestre would give us the Grand Canal plus quiet, comfortable sleep in a room with cable TV and a private bath with a hair dryer. My sister, the corporate traveler on whose frequent flyer miles we had flown, was grumpy about the location. All this frugality had to be rewarded somehow, and she decided it would be on Bellinis at Harry's Bar in Venice on the Grand Canal.

Well, that was our Alamo, our Saigon, our Tikrit. Sixteen Euros for a peach juice and champagne cocktail. After drinking one apiece, neither of us felt a buzz. We were sober enough to do the math: at that day's exchange rate, each Bellini had cost $22.46. We scurried out of Harry's, regretting whatever Yankee arrogance or stupidity had led us there in the first place.

From then on, the Bellini became our point of reference for everything. In Mestre, we indulged in three-course dinners with wine, proclaiming, "This whole meal cost less than that Bellini." An ornate Venetian mask was just "a few more Euros than a Bellini." Laced espadrille shoes were "cheaper than a Bellini." We calculated our cab fare and tip to the airport at "about two Bellinis."

Last week, my sister called me from a bar in Half Moon Bay, a sort of Mestre to our hometown, San Francisco. She informed me that she was looking out at the wide, blue ocean and drinking a Bellini that cost less than half of what we'd paid in Venice. And yes, this time, she was buzzed.

I'm a Long Way from Home

Patricia Oropeza, mentor

My mentee, Marylou, and I meet at Barnes & Noble to write. During one session we went to the music section and picked out interesting song titles, including "I'm a Long Way From Home" from the Walk the Line soundtrack. Just one phrase can really get your mind going and your hand writing.

As I got on the bus, I slowly turned my head to get one last glimpse. I was about to leave my home behind, the only place I'd lived and known since I was born 20 years ago. I swallowed hard and blinked to hold back the tears. I had thought about this for a long time, debating whether or not to do it, but now that I was at the bus station I knew I was doing the right thing. I couldn't stay here. It was too hard being in this town. Everything was a reminder of what had happened. I didn't want to deal with any of these thoughts and feelings anymore. Ever since my dad had died, I couldn't handle everyone telling me how sorry they were; looking at me with what I felt was pity. That's why I was going a long way from home. I was heading to California, where no one knew me or my family or anything about me. I had some money I had saved through the years, so I was able to buy my bus ticket and even had a few hundred dollars left over. Once I got to Cali I'd find a job waitressing or something. I sighed and climbed the bus stairs. I plopped myself down on a seat. I knew I was doing the best thing for me. Being a long way from home would do me lots of good.

The Raffle Ticket

Vicki Biegner, age 16

"Welcome to Heaven," says God, "Now, for the records, tell me how you died."

Well, it all started when a Girl Scout knocked on my door asking if I would like to buy a raffle ticket to win two roundtrips to Asia. I was in a good mood so I bought one, just to be nice. Weeks went by, and I completely forgot about the raffle ticket until early one morning (a little too early for me), when I got a phone call from Willow, the Girl Scout leader. She told me (a little too enthusiastically) that I was the lucky winner of the Trip to Asia raffle. I told her I didn't want it, to choose another raffle ticket, but that Willow was a persistent one. She would not take no for an answer. She told me to pick up the tickets at the airport and assured me it would be a wonderful experience. Reluctantly, I called my sister and told her to pack her bags; we were going to Asia. I most certainly wasn't going alone.

We arrived in China after the 15-hour flight with two layovers in Tokyo and Moscow. Culture shock set in immediately, and we got lost within minutes. We knocked on a red door that looked friendly. A woman in a flowered dress opened the door and though she spoke no English, she welcomed us with open arms. We spoke through gestures and the help of the Chinese-English dictionary I had picked up in the airport. She invited us to stay with her for the night, so we squeezed into a room smaller than my closet and already inhabited by three small children. Jetlag set in, and we were knocked out in minutes.

The following morning the welcoming woman, named Lee, already had breakfast on the table. My sister and I couldn't name a single dish, but decided to eat out of respect. I took a bite of the yellowish-blue egg-like concoction. It tasted like a mix of old rubber tires and moldy cheese. We thanked Lee for her warm hospitality, but were not sad to be moving on.

Back on the streets, I called Willow with the number she gave me to use in case of an emergency. I asked her how I was supposed to get around in a country I knew nothing about. She replied, "The way will find you if you let it," whatever that was supposed to mean. Frustrated, I turned to my sister whose mouth dropped. "Your face is turning purple!!!" She screamed. I raced through my Gucci purse looking for my compact and fainted when I saw the purple color taking over my face.

When I woke up I was in a hospital with seven doctors crouched over me, poking and screaming at each other in Chinese. When they saw that I was awake, they dispersed like a school of fish witnessing a shark. In came Dr. Smith, a big man with oversized glasses, a curly mustache, and a clipboard in his hand. He immediately began questioning me without introducing himself. He scowled and asked where I was from. I whispered that I was from the United States. He asked how long I had been here, and I told him barely one day, as tears flooded my eyes. Then he asked me what I had eaten. Now I was stumped, but I was scared not to answer this intimidating man. I told him that I actually didn't know — a woman gave me breakfast, but I wasn't quite sure what it was.

He asked me if I eat food without knowing what it is. A rhetorical question, I assumed. He walked out for ten minutes, and when he came back he told me I had contracted the bird flu.

God interrupts my story to ask if I died from the bird flu. I tell him no, I recovered after a week in the hospital and returned home. Once I was back in the States, Oprah wanted to interview me about of my harrowing journey. After the interview I was driving home and a flock of birds flew right into my windshield. I crashed into a tree and my airbags didn't go off, and that is how I came to grace God with my presence.

God says, "Well, birds seemed to really have it out for you." I actually blame the Girl Scouts.

I wrote this during a mentoring session on places we had visited.

Arriving in Paradise

Amaree Tanawong, mentor

Breathing in the climate, I feel the
humidity hit my skin.

Green hills, narrow dirt roads,
Motorbikes everywhere.
Families of four sit on a scooter.
The father in front,
The mother in back,
Two children holding on,
Squashed in the middle.

I am seated in an air-conditioned van,
Staring out the window.
Nobody stares back.
My name-brand luggage in the trunk,
A designer purse on my lap,
I'm an all too common tourist.

Fascinated by the store signs, the foreign
Characters, the tin roofs,
Eager to walk on the streets and
Speak with the locals.

We turn south, moving away from the
Small towns,
I see the ocean — not the deep
Blue of the Pacific, but the
Crystal green hue of the Andaman Sea.
High-rise hotels pop up on the landscape.

The driver slows the car, pulling
Into the hotel's circular driveway.
We are escorted to our room.
I step onto the balcony —
The ocean stares at me.
I look down, spot the pool and a sea of
White Europeans.

The brown roads and green trees of
The Island have disappeared.
All I see now are the white sands and
White tourists.

Write in different places. Keep a notebook. Write in a park or on a street-corner or in an alley. You don't have to write about the place, but it will influence your writing.

Write alone by a green lake.

The River

Abby Anderson, mentor

This is a piece I wrote in 1992 after my mom and I took a mother-daughter trip to Costa Rica. It has added significance for me now since my mom died of cancer in 2002. I read it at our WriteGirl Out Loud event at Dutton's Books. I know Mom, who worked as a teacher and at a children's bookstore, would be crazy about WriteGirl.

We stared at the river in amazement. We were alone, two women, visitors in a country where the language sounded to us like strange and beautiful music, a song we did not know.

My mother was driving, and I was her navigator. On my lap, the Lonely Planet guide lay open to the page that simply read, "Cross two rivers, then continue up the hill." Those were the only directions — entirely neglecting to mention the absence of a bridge. The obstacle of the river was very real, since our beds for the night at the Arenal Volcano Observatory lay at the top of the hill on the other side of the river.

Our little blue Subaru rental at once seemed inadequate. It had the added oddity of being the exact same color, year and model as every other rental car on the road in the entire country, part of an aimless wandering army of tourists.

We sat contemplating, the windows rolled down, hoping in vain to catch some moving air to compensate for the tropical heat. The only sound was a strange whispering that drifted out of the shady jungle that surrounded us. Officially, the rainy season had begun, but so far there'd been no rain. The river didn't seem to know that, though, judging by its bounty.

Suddenly, another car passed us. It barreled fearlessly through the water, splashing up a funnel of spray.

The brazenness of this unseen driver did not tell us how deep the water was or whether our Subaru could swim, but at least it assured us of one thing: it was possible. A silent look passed between us. A sudden revving of the Subaru's brave little motor, and we were off.

We have no photo of the river. In the moment of experience, we neglected to get out the camera. It's just as well because now, years later, it is a stronger memory than any of the places we immortalized on film. Like the photos of microscopic toucans we saw so vividly in real life, the river may well have looked like a meaningless trickle.

When we came home, the story simply became further proof of our friend's assertion that, "Abby and Kathy go to places with weird bugs!" An anecdote for dinner parties. Yet, to me, this journey came to symbolize the bravery with which we face the smaller events of daily life. As with many of the challenges we overcome, in the end, it is the triumph we remember, not the struggle. I can't actually recall being in the midst of all that water, only reaching the other side. The river was more than a bit of water, more than an inconvenience in our well-made travel plans. It reaffirmed our hidden strength as women and our bond as mother and daughter.

Chapter 9 { Home }

The Contents of Our Closets

The scents and sounds of home
can be powerful sources of inspiration.

Plans for the Rose in the Middle

Stephanie M. Almendarez, age 18

I was in my bedroom trying to write something and feeling stuck when my mother called me outside to eat dinner on our porch. I decided a change of scenery would help my writing. Then I picked up Nothing Held Back and came across "Observations on a Rainy Day." I let my eyes sweep from left to right, up and down, and wrote about what I saw and how I felt.

Only three red roses were born on the bush in the garden. Their leaves were like penguins waddling in the cold wind. The shortest-stemmed rose dangled almost to the grass, as if it were ready to puke some seeds. The rose in the middle is just like me. We were both born in between, and we are both in my picture. I am wearing a green tank top and black Dickies. And we are both indifferent in our not in, not out kind of way. The tallest rose's face is touched by one of the enormous pine tree's branches, like those fingers from Michelangelo's ceiling painting. The song of a flying bird and the sound of someone hammering mix together with the sound of my mother shaking her gold spray-paint can; it sounds like a metal toy is stuck inside it. She is painting two angel curtain-rod brackets. I kind of like the strong smell of the gold spray-paint, just like I don't despise the smell of gasoline and nail polish. My mom does, though.

On the sidewalk across the street from my house, a little Hispanic boy rides on the back of his older brother's bicycle. They are both laughing. A little black boy with glasses and a blue t-shirt is dancing like Michael Jackson, his palms dropping and rising in waves. The sun was shining a few minutes ago on the grass of the house to my left, where a bunch of kids are playing and shouting like crazy. My mother told me a few minutes ago that if my brother and sister and I were still little, we would surely be playing with those kids — eramos "engavillados."

The church bells have just rung. I've gotten so used to their sound that they don't inspire me anymore. Only occasionally, when they play the Ave Maria, will I stop and listen.

I guess Mom's right. I would be playing over there with those kids if I were still seven, or eight, or nine, or something. But I'm not. I'm eighteen, and I have no boyfriend. Growing up is boring. I haven't even gone to a club yet. But then again, I'm not the dancing type.

The sun is setting from behind the church steeple. The clouds are orange and pink and purple. Cars race by; it's Saturday night. And I don't even have plans yet. But then again, Saturday night is only a Saturday night, and do I ever have plans?

Monsieur Clown

Alejandra Cardenas, age 13

He's stuck forever

and his thoughts seem reflected

on his face

Sorrowful bliss

or blissful sorrow, I don't know

The paint seems to be purposely faded, as if

to show delicacy

Large sections of French newspaper — old, worn,

and brown — protrude from it and blend with it at

the same time

The sad clown, as though in an act of desperation,

grabbed what he could in order to stay in touch with

his French roots

Though he seems to be sleeping, I know he can hear me

Good night, monsieur, good night.

Boyfriend in a Box

Melissa Anderson Sweazy, mentor

At the Creative Nonfiction Workshop, we were asked to describe the contents of our closet. The process of discovery was exciting; I unleashed some potent material I could develop into a longer piece.

I'm married, but I keep my boyfriends stacked in the closet. No longer a physical presence in my life, they have been reduced down to ephemera — movie stubs, dried rose petals that made each one, at one time, my entire universe. My first Mr. Universe lives in the L.L. Bean box that came with the cowboy boots he bought for junior prom. In the box is an American flag bandana I begged him to let me wear so I could assert my Southern pride. He dumped me shortly after prom, but he let me keep the bandana. Then there is the Josh Box, formerly home to my gold sequined heels that now is packed to the brim with origami-quality folded notes — the way we communicated before the days of text messages and IM-ing. The notes largely concerned themselves with talks of prom and field parties from girls named April and Heather, weird inside jokes involving carpooling to the mall and a red tunic top from Express. Some of the notes wondered if Josh and I might be headed down the aisle one day. The felt ring box I fished out from under the notes confirmed it. Eighteen with a promise ring. I can only imagine my parents' sweet relief the day he tugged the ring off my finger and stormed away in tears. Andrew is buried in the Tiffany's box, and peering inside it, I was happy to find that my heart had tunneled its way out. I quickly shut that one, not wanting to let any ghosts escape, just to be safe.

The Things I Save

Steph Opitz, mentor

This was inspired by an experiment on the things we save — in this case, a letter. I learned that there are many positive things about not becoming what you wanted to be when you grew up.

Sifting through boxes of old dance costumes and art projects while cleaning out my mom's storage space on my last visit home, I happened upon a box of saved knick-knacks. Just before throwing it out in hopes of hurrying along the day's work, I noticed a pile of notes passed among my friends in junior high. Under that pile I found my single-use headgear from fifth grade (my brother Scott made a disparaging comment about my weight and the contraption over my mouth that, although I laugh about it now, I never got over), and next to that, a time capsule. The time capsule intrigued me. Written cautiously on the outside it said, "Do not open until 1997!!" Overshooting the warning by eight years, I eagerly opened the capsule. Inside, deteriorating wide-lined paper held words I had crafted in a different world where I had problems like recruiting neighbors to play sardines, choosing between pink or black ballet slippers, and the most pressing concern, whether the Minnesota Twins would win the 1991 World Series. In faded pencil etching I addressed this particular issue in a poem titled "Win Twins." After the '87 World Series victory, I became an avid Twins fan by mathematical deduction: my dad and brothers loved baseball and they were cool; therefore, coolness must correlate with baseball. I rehearsed stats and sportscaster commentary I didn't understand just to impress my family. I'll never forget the look on my brother Craig's face when I articulated concern for the slump Chili Davis had found himself in. My other brother, Scott, though, was less enthusiastic about my company at the games. Rolled up with the Twins homage, I found a letter expressing my relationship with Scott, among other concerns. The letter asked, "Dear Steph, or are you going by Stephanie now? How's life? Are you drinking or using drugs? If yes, you should stop. They are bad. Is Scott still a jerk?" and so on. As I read through my nine year-old observations on life, I realized I still have a long path ahead to reach the goals I'd dreamt up for myself. My 21st birthday dismantled my drinking caveat, I hadn't become a professional ballerina, and I haven't taken any giant leaps in world peace. And still, I know that Steph would be proud of the present Steph (not Stephanie). I graduated college, went on to graduate school, explored many parts of the world, and I am surrounded by people who love me. I have long given up trying to find cohorts for night games, the Twins will never be the same for me after Kirby Puckett, and I actually get along with my brothers; I am nothing that I thought I would be, and yet I'm saving the capsule. It reminds me not of the things I failed to achieve, but that although I am different from what I'd dreamt, the third grade Steph would still think I am cool.

The Garden

Allegra Calderon, age 18

My mentor and I were inspired by a WriteGirl workshop to write about a favorite place. I chose a place where I feel safe, a place that I love.

The window isn't big enough, but the cat goes in and out as I sit, lie, walk, roll, jump, pace, and sleep in this room. The corners seem dirty. Spiders always like corners. Dust collects. The window is next to the bed. A Christmas light canopy hangs overhead.

Katherine says the room feels like a garden — with a bed, computers, wardrobe, stereo, and books. Perfect. The window opens and lets the outside in. The walls are green, so I can understand why she calls it a garden.

The rain beats against our bedroom window and makes a calm sound as I sleep. My furry companion sits in the chair, one eye opened. Now that the computer is off, the rain is all that's heard, and it disturbs her sleep. But not mine. The blue light reflecting off the stereo makes the perfect, luminescent backdrop for calming rain in my fictional garden.

My Studio

The piece shows my conflicting feelings about my workspace. I followed some good writing advice: explore the source of dissatisfaction in order to create a story.

Susan A. Kitchens, mentor

I spend more waking hours in my home studio than anywhere else. I'm tempted to describe it by listing all the computers: the huge ninety-pound monitor on top of my big desk, the silver PowerMac underneath, the two cute little computers high on bookshelves (a backup server, a web server), the corner desk with the lesser monitor for the Windoze box, my sickly old house-bound PowerBook, the old PowerMac that I can't bear to get rid of, and all the wires and routers that snake under the desk to connect these computers to the printer, each other, and the world. But I'm bored by my catalog of silicon and wires and magnetic media.

This room holds projects and messes, promise and despair. I scrawl ideas onto big sheets of butcher paper taped to the closet doors. A few days ago I emptied a carry-bag onto the floor to repack it with camera and sound equipment for the WriteGirl workshop; I need to stop stepping over it and put things away. Behind me, my drawing table is piled high with files and papers, good intentions and old taxes, and that bookbinding project I began last year. Plants by the window give me something nice to see besides the stucco of the next condo building. Those plants need water; I should trim their dead leaves.

For all my time here, I don't see the rest of the room. My vision narrows to the rectangular glow on my desk. I stare into the phosphorescent tunnel. It draws me into overlapping windows of text and pixels, typography and sound waves, movies and HTML code. And email and spam. Always spam. The blogs I follow with soap opera addiction whisper, "Stop what you're doing. Just for a moment. Is there anything new? Who's updated their site?" Two hours later, I blink my eyes. Now, where was I?

My Fellowship

Jazmine Yuba, age 17

When my mentor asked me to write about a place where I spend a lot of time, I chose my bedroom. Clearly, I have an overactive imagination and, as a senior in high school, I'm rebelling against boring homework!

Timed writing. I hate these the most. Here I am, sitting at my desk, trying to do this...thing. "Read the passage and analyze blah blah blah." God, I'm already losing interest. Ho, hum. Just try to ignore it, Jaz. Twirl about in your chair. Look about the room. Don't look at the desk. Spin around in the chair. Don't look at the desk. Why must I be cursed to do such meaningless junk? Just go 'round and 'round in your comfy computer chair and look at the top of your dresser.

Hang on. Why's Frodo far away from Sam? I'll fix that. There you go, ring bearer, back to your trusted companion. Hmmm...Legolas's bow is missing. What did you do with it Aragorn? You won't talk, huh? Oh, that's a big mistake. Now you and the hobbits will have to fight, four against one. Bwahahahaha! Take that you mangy ranger! Yeah, we're winning! Aragorn is on the floor, defeated. Gather 'round my hobbit pals. Let us celebrate our victory and — Pippin! Stop kicking the poor guy, all right? That's not cool.

Knock-knock.

Uh oh. Quickly men! Back to your places. Straighten up the desk, Jaz. Grab the pen and write. "Come in!" Plaster on a fake smile.

"Oh hi, Mom. No I'm just working on a paper — nothing too exciting. Yes, I'm almost done. Bye. Yes, I'm sure I wasn't yelling." Phew, that was a close one.

Now, where was I? Oh yeah! Merry, hand me Legolas's bow. Thank you. Ahem. Oh sexy elfin prince, the hobbit foursome and I have toiled arduously to return your beloved weapon. Oh, you're too kind, Legolas. You flatter me so. Oh dear heavens — me? The most beautiful creature your eyes have ever beheld? Clearly you jest. Yes, I'm single. Why do you ask? Oh, Legolas! Me, on a romantic date with you? I think I feel faint. Wow, I really should be doing my work, so it seems we must depart for now. Now don't give me that look. You know I could never leave you. Of course I'll hurry back. This is my room, after all. Gee Leggy, don't embarrass me in front of the others. Okay, one quick kiss. Happy? That's good. Time for me to get back to work. Goodbye my Fellowship.

Turn the chair around, Jaz. Back to the desk. Face the essay.

Once I Lost a Set of Keys

Marlys West, mentor

Once I lost a set of keys

and did not know the magic words

that yank things back

from the long, sighing hallway of lost necessities

and treasures.

I circled my locked house but could not get in.

The phone began ringing: a long-lost friend,

my husband needing a ride home again.

Black phone close by the kitchen window

and me too scared to break in.

Crying for keys makes your eyeteeth sparkle.

It's like crying for the movie ticket bought

and immediately lost.

You might as well not.

Chaos loves the stuck lock

and stubbed toe, diamonds falling from rings,

sun winking over the tumbling stone.

Chaos will snatch things up and run along

whispering bad thanks

for the just-broken prong.

A filing system is non-existent.

My keys rest near two colored pencils the artist most

needed, under false teeth stashed

in a red-striped sock in a box hidden under the last

room's sheetrock

and bag of fallen gravel

by a certain bird fossil that would have proven

infinitely useful to the ornithologists.

My writing space is my bed. I write in a down comforter nest.
I consider it a sacred space.

Write at 4 a.m.
Everything is so peaceful that many worlds can unfold.

Chapter 10 { Tall Tales }

Look for the
Nearest Cubbyhole

tall tales tall tales tall tales tall tales tall tales tall tales tall tales tall tales tall tales tall tales tall tales tall tales tall tales tall tales tall tales tall tales tall tales tall tales tall tales tall tales

Try having your characters do the unexpected. You can always hit "delete."

A blank page means there's nothing there. You have to make up
the whole thing: every street corner, car door, every person,
place and thing. It's scary and wonderful.

Forget yourself, be someone else.

Don't be anthrocentric; animals, objects and
others have a story to tell too.

Take five minutes

before writing to meditate and inhabit your

characters so you can write from their perspective.

You have ideas spinning around in your head that need to be set free.

Fire

Portia J. Frazier, age 15

I sat watching the fire my mom made for about an hour as it tried to exploit every crack in the wood. If it couldn't burn through, it would dig a hole through the center.

It laps at the sides of its prey

peeling its way inside

delighting in the screams

feasting on their tears

branding its possession

on the body not its own

carving out a place to hide

when the wind breathes its name

dancing on their graves

flowing like heated silk

laughing at the dark

and at war with the cold.

My mentor, Jennifer, and I edited this together,
working on word choice, economy and surprise.

Hellfire

Morgan Miller, age 14

It was a stormy night, but there were no bright flashes of lightning or menacing cackles of thunder. Abidee, Travis and I were trotting down the cobble-decorated road. Travis wrapped his arms around his wife as I inhaled the scent of the icy wind. Then I heard something creep through the blue bushes. My sharp-tuned ears picked up a sound, the sound of terror. And I smelled a unique odor: the odor of death.

I froze and barked a warning to the stealthy enemy. The bushes stopped rattling. Travis and Abidee paused their flirting and glanced at me, their pale eyes shining with worry.

"Diamond, what's the matter, girl?" Travis whispered, bending to my level. Abidee was white as a blank piece of paper. Then he sauntered into the pale lighting of the pregnant moon. What was that hellhound doing here? I knew who he was — Old Man Worl's companion. His name was Hellfire, and he had the reputation to prove it. His muscular body seemed sculpted out of solid rock, and he only had one eye. He was uninterested in me — a bird-like Afghan — even though I instinctively curled my black lips and exposed my fangs, threatening to maul his eye out. He circled me to go to Abidee, staring at her shuddering form, his only eye digging into her very soul. Then he positioned himself to…No! He was going to attack her!

I tugged against my leash, but Travis wasn't getting my signal; he just stood there, horrified. I had to do this myself. If Hellfire wanted to inflict harm on my family, he was going to have to kill me first. He leapt towards Abidee, but I managed to bat him away. He got up slowly and confidently, like he'd anticipated my move. He looked at me and I saw only one thing in his red eye: unbridled anger.

Then he was scratching my face, ripping my right ear into hairy pieces. I yelped as the blood started to trickle, small drops of red liquid staining the cobblestones. Hellfire backed away, watching me react to my searing pain. I lunged at him, my forelegs pinning his back to the cold ground. I had his thick neck clamped in my mouth; I felt his jaw's grip lighten up on my tail.
I noticed that we were on top of a long, rough hill. Suddenly, I had an idea. I wrestled him close to the edge. Then, my back legs flung his dark body off of me. He fell to the bottom of the hill with a sickening crack. I knew he was dead; no canine could live through that.

The fingers of the wind caressed my matted and stained fur. I looked up at the glowing orb in the night sky and let out a raspy howl, celebrating my victory and telling my tale to friends. Then darkness surrounded me as I collapsed to the ground.

Hyakutake's Comet

Tracy Chait, mentor

I shouldn't have looked. I should have listened to my inner third grade teacher, my inner ophthalmologist. Trouble was, I don't really have an inner third grade teacher or, until recently, much concern about my vision. When Hyakutake made its fiery pass through the heavens in the almost-spring of 1996 I was all eyes. Sure, I'd heard the old wives' tales. I thought about making one of those pinhole boxes you learn to craft in elementary school to view the various eclipses. Maybe I just got lazy. Maybe I wanted to put myself in danger. Maybe it was some kind of oedipal self-fulfilling prophecy (ideally without the incest). At this point, it's hard to divine why I chose to put myself in harm's way like that. They say hindsight is 20-20. I'd argue, not quite.

There were no initial symptoms. The night of Hyakutake's first appearance, I was alone on my roof deck. There were no viewing parties like Hale-Bopp got, where people toted along brie and soprasetta to friends' houses in Newton. There were no toasts or make-your-own-eye-protector sessions. I happened to read about Hyakutake in that morning's Boston Globe. It was a Monday, the day of the special Science section. Just a small column on page B-3: 7:38 p.m., look sixteen degrees Southeast of Venus. I happened to be home at that time, and my roommates were all watching the game at a friend's place. I cruised to the roofdeck, and I guess I figured "What the heck?" The thing wasn't going to come around for another 73 years. Hyakutake arrived in mid-March, and according to NASA's reports, it would be naked-eye visible for at least two months.

After that first observation, I started wondering if Hyakutake got jealous of Haley, or, if the name had been easier to pronounce, would the comet have gotten better PR. I felt some kind of kinship to Hyakutake, and since no one was talking about his comet, I started to feel a responsibility to it. With me, it attained a certain "if a tree falls in the forest" status, like if I wasn't going to go up on the roofdeck and check it out, maybe all the hard work that Japanese guy did wouldn't exist. I spent the whole of early spring 1996 viewing Hyakutake. It was something I felt compelled to show up for, like picking up your kid after school or remembering to get your oil changed. Much like filing my taxes in January, watching Hyakutake was a task I could feel competitively virtuous about doing.

tall tales

175

Alternate Narnia

Tanja Laden, mentor

My mentee, Karen, and I used the song titles of the Narnia soundtrack to create pieces that were uniquely our own. We learned that we have different ways of using the same words; I wrote a poem while Karen wrote a short story.

Poor Lucy, wunderkind,

percolating with lullabies

in the blitz.

Battling the winter abyss,

evacuating the woods

for adventurous London.

Sees Father knighting the stony witch.

Sees his table, takes it all in,

spends her White Christmas with him.

Planning her lighting wardrobe, can't wait to begin.

Meditation

Karen Toledo, age 13

I was sitting on cool, green grass covered in dew, meditating. A small river was in front of me. Nothing swam in it. And there were small candles floating on the surface. Everything was quiet, and the sky was grey and cloudy. A raven landed on a lifeless tree. I heard a foal and its mother across the river. They stopped to get a drink of water then galloped away. Then I heard large, powerful wings in the sky. It was Pegasus, and he landed in front of me; I could feel his breath on my face. He knew I was harmless, so he plucked a feather off his beautiful wing for me and flew away. Then the feather landed on my lap. I could feel its energy, so powerful and so warm.

Suddenly, I heard footsteps; I didn't open my eyes. Then I felt someone's hands take my shoulders and lift me up. I opened my eyes. It was him — the guy I liked! I looked into his eyes, a beautiful shade of brown. I put my hands on his cheeks, and our lips drew together. He stopped at 90%, and I completed the other 10%. I wrapped my arms around his neck and we fell into the river. Then we turned into koi fishes — one black, and one white. We swam in a circle and made the sign of Yin and Yang.

I looked up and saw a girl meditating. She had a feather on her lap.

This comes from a story challenge that my mentor Marlen and I made up – to write a story about finding a purse – and searching for the owner.

The Private Purse Investigator

Sara Kaye Larson, mentor

I was on the 309 bus on a Tuesday afternoon in August. I was coming home from a dead-end case, and I was worried about how I was going to pay rent this month. I had only been a private investigator for two months and my partner, the one with all the tech equipment (and car), had already left me. I must have been cursed. Well, I should have known I was cursed. How many PIs ride the bus in Los Angeles?

I got to sit next to this real fidgety woman who was wearing a large winter coat in the middle of August. Maybe she didn't want to lose it. I know people like that. People that keep all their possessions on them at all times. This woman kept scratching her head, and it made me nervous. Maybe she had bugs. I wanted to break away from her and the bugs, but this bus was crowded. I had reached the end of my rope when the bus stopped and the lady got up and waddled off, scratching her head the whole time.

I was so happy to have the whole bench to myself, but that only lasted a second. This young punk pushed through and stole the space next to me. I thought I had another bug-filled passenger to deal with when he reached under his bum (you can imagine how grossed out I was by this time), and pulled a big knapsack made from a vintage tablecloth, looking at me with that "Is this yours?" look.

How I longed to be someone that looked so intimidating and so obviously a private investigator that no one would dare sit next to me, let alone ask if a poppy-patterned purse was mine. My day was already on the slide so I grabbed the purse with careful hands (worried that the old lady might have left bugs on it). I took a quick peek inside and saw wads and wads of paper.

Holy cow. I have struck it rich, I thought.

I couldn't wait to get off at the next stop. But I knew from my PI training that you couldn't make sudden suspicious movements. The young punk might have been tipped off that something profitable was going on. I lost my professional composure and got off at the next stop anyway.

I had to be alone with that bag!

I looked for the nearest cubbyhole, a place that would be good to count my cash. I found one by a 98-Cent store that was no longer open. I surveyed (PI speak for looking around) that area and when I decided it was safe enough I crouched down and opened the bag. My first handful of "bills" turned out to be carefully cut coupons for Cap'n Crunch! There were over a hundred of them, some expired and some from Sunday's newspaper. The rest of the bag was filled with carefully cut coupons all organized by brand. What was the meaning of this?

I searched for some contact info but found only a solitary Ralphs grocery store card. I headed for the first Ralphs I could find.

The Purse

Marlen Reyes, age 13

"Mom, I'm tired of shopping," I said.

It's hard to go shopping with my mother because she always wants everything.

"I propose that you only shop for 30 minutes," I said.

"No mas callate," Mom said, shutting me up.

"Mommy, I'm going to the restroom, OK?" I told her laughing.

On the way to the restroom, I bumped into a tall lady dressed in black. She stood there staring at me so I stared back. You could barely see her green eyes. She had blonde hair, but she dyed it black with royal blue. I could say that she was at least 6 foot 3 inches tall. She was white – really white.

"What are you staring at, little girl?" The Lady said to me. "Leonora, let's go." A man was with her. They ran out. When I turned to look at the basket I saw a purse. The lady named Leonora left her purse.

"Lady, lady," I said, running after her. "You forgot your purse!" I ran out of the store but couldn't reach her because she was already at her car. It looked like she'd fled from something or someone. So I walked back to the supermarket to go into the bathroom. I got to thinking about why she had fled.

When I got to my mom she asked, "Where did you get that purse from?"

"Well, this lady, I think her name was Leonora, and she dropped it, and we can take it back to her and…and…"

"And what?" Mom managed to ask.

"And we can take it back to her. Do you think we can?" I asked.

"Sorry, I can't. You know I am very busy, and I can't."

Later that afternoon I took off, trying to find the lady. I went outside to call my cousin Stacy. She loves to solve mysteries.

"Staz, I got one! Do you want to help?" I asked her.

"Of course. What's it about? A purse?" she asked.

"How do you manage to always figure out what it's about? Are you a witch?" I asked and hung up.

I went into the purse. The purse had an ID with a picture of her and her information, a check, a real gun, a fake ID with her picture glued to it (the name on it was Adriana Cobra), and a paper that had records of her crimes! It had five crimes on it!

Stacy finally came over, and I told her, "We have never had a mystery this big." I handed her the purse and she froze.

*This grew out of the character experiment we did at a
workshop and it is my first attempt at creative nonfiction.*

Fear of Water

Michelle Lewis, mentor

The constant door buzzing is making Truman's teeth hurt. Short blasts of carbon monoxide through the open window slap him in the face and he leans away. Reesa is on the sidewalk below, shouting up insults.

Must…get…up (Loser!)
Must…stop…buzzing (Wimp!)
Please…make…it…stop (Scumbag!)

Buzz, buzz, buzzing.

The tile floor turns to liquid beneath him – shifting shapes and reflections on top of a bottomless sea. The sofa rocks like a small raft.

The crash of a wave (a truck over a pothole).
A foghorn (a car honking at a bike messenger).

Truman presses his eyelids shut to cast out this scene he has created. He didn't actually see his father's car go over the side of the small bridge, but he knows exactly what it felt like. Tasting sand and salty wetness up his nose until it runs down the back of his throat like acid. Gasping for one last breath. Staring up at the grey water over glass, sharp cold like pins and needles working their way up, up, up, flash freezing each inch of skin into permanent numbness. Then clarity. Then nothing.

He takes a deep swallow of air, holds his nose and tumbles off the couch. Waiting to sink, his body stops short. He is in the fetal position on the floor of his apartment and Truman registers this, "Oh, right." But still he decides it's safer to swim. Stretching his body out long, he begins to kick his legs and breaststroke his arms out in front of him. Taking measured breaths, he wriggles and paddles his way across the living room floor towards the door. Through his water filled eyes, he understands there is a coat hanger several feet before him, but decides it is a buoy and thinks I'll never make it that far!

Buzz. (Come on, you jerk!!! Open the door!)

Between Places

Jacqueline Jaffe, mentor

Paul leans on the horn again. He's not impatient; the sound just makes him happy. It's so loud and brassy, the way it blasts through the morning air, honk, honk, like a crazy goose in heat. Through the spanking new windshield, Paul can see clear out to the San Gabriel foothills. Hopeful weather, Paul feels, as the Santa Anas kick up dust. Debris skitters and palms sway up and down San Vicente Boulevard — a good day for a road trip.

Paul double-parks outside his cousin Mike's building. When another big car whizzes by, he honks again, not necessarily to rouse Michael, but more as a greeting from one car to another. Paul has just leased the shiny black Cadillac, anthracite to be exact. When he first spied it, center stage on the floor of the showroom, it brought back memories. Sam, his father, used to drive a bigger boat than this one back in the sixties when Paul was a teenager. What Paul loved the most about the old Caddy were its cracked red leather seats. Lipstick red, he recalls, maybe because of all the make-out sessions conducted in the back seat.

Paul considers it a point of honor to lease a new car each year no matter how much he's in over his head. Last year, it was a forest green Land Rover, the year before that, a silver Porsche. This time out, he was looking for something solid, familiar. Sam taught him that it's the car, not the clothes that make the man. None of the guys he knows care about what kind of label is sticking out of your shirt

What clinched the deal was all that cargo room. Recently, through a series of bad breaks, Paul's lost everything — the beach house, the business, even the girlfriend who saw him through the divorce. He's between places at the moment. He sleeps in the guesthouse behind his friend Stewart's place in the Palisades. What little his ex left behind, he dumped up at the big landfill on Mulholland, overlooking the Valley. He keeps a duffle packed with a fresh set of clothes, his toothbrush, a bar of Ivory, and an oversized towel in the trunk, in case he winds up somewhere other than Stewart's at the end of the day. His mother, Sarah, would turn over in her grave if she only knew. And what would Ellie think? He can just picture his ex-wife throwing her slender neck back and letting out one of her signature snorts.

But Paul feels pared down, sleek as a Swiss Army knife, without the excess baggage. What more does a guy need than a new set of wheels and a cell phone? He can conduct business tooling down the 405, and he gets to keep moving.

And Now a Story about Two Fools that Go into the Haunted Zoo at a Very Inopportune Time!

Sara Kaye Larson, mentor

This piece was inspired by my mentee Marlen's love of fiction and my love of Griffith Park. This piece comes from an experiment titled "Describe a Haunted Place."

To our sweet young couple Tammy and Tim, it seemed like a normal day and certainly a good day for a bike ride in a city park. What they didn't know (or care to ask their super-natural almanac) was that very day, December 7th, was Animal Torture Remembrance Day, and it was considered evil and dangerous to go near any spot where an animal had been held in captivity or tortured.

How were they supposed to know there used to be a zoo in Griffith Park? There was supposed to be an observatory, but they couldn't find that either. So they just pedaled along the rolling trails of hard-packed Los Angeles earth, Tim on his blue bike and Tammy on her pink one.

Their trail grew less and less populated with other bikers, but neither of them took notice. Not because they were sick in love or anything. It was most likely because it wasn't quiet. Not in the least. Tim's soundscape remained the same whether he was in an airplane hanger or in nature as long as Tammy was around. You see, Tammy had a habit of talking a lot. So Tim would just pedal and take a drink out of his rubber sport squirt bottle every so often and then put it back in the metal wire rack. He took 43 squirt sips in the time it took Tammy to discuss the new Harry Potter movie and Christmas shopping. So you can imagine that as soon as Tim heard the near complete relaxing silence of the wind gently agitating the leaves, he knew something was terribly wrong. Tammy was gone.

"Tammy!"

Tim looked this way and that, and she was nowhere to be found. Luckily he was properly hydrated and was able to pedal swiftly back down the hill he and his sweet one had just climbed. Before he even reached the bottom he saw her pink ten-speed lying on the ground. His heart sank. His squeeze bottle fell off his bike and rolled a few feet to the entrance of a cave he hadn't noticed before. He looked up and there she was!

"Tammy!"

She just stood there like she didn't hear him.

"Tammy!" He ran toward her.

Tammy couldn't stop staring into the cave. She started to cry and held her hands over her ears as if she couldn't stand to hear Tim yell her name.

He grabbed her shoulders.

"Tammy — what is the matter?! What are you staring at?" He looked in the direction that had her so mesmerized. And just then he heard it. Oh it was so sad. He couldn't stand to hear it anymore, and he wanted to take Tammy and get out but he couldn't move.

Tim covered his ears, but he could still hear it. The sound was getting sadder and sadder by the minute. He longed for his water bottle, but he couldn't even move his head to look at his little buttercup. The young fools had fallen into the paralyzing sadness of the tortured mother bear.

Chapter 11 {Tributes}

A Face of a Thousand Stories

Write what you love, love what you write.

Try to capture someone you admire with imagery.
Show, don't tell, what makes them special.

Who are the heroes in your world?

Pupusas

Melissa Castillo, age 15

Two choices, beans or cheese,

one tortilla with filling.

My grandmother gathers dough

that weighs more than her frail body.

She smiles as if to show her independence

then smashes the dough as if it were all the problems of the world.

She softly rolls it and thins it out as if it were her children.

She pours the filling as if it were a magical vice.

She cooks it until its intoxicating smell

runs through the house and gathers

her children home. She serves it as if saying,

I am still the mother.

Her secret power, her life, her dish, her magical food

reunites a separated family.

Her legacy and my inheritance.

V.I.P. List

Stephanie M. Almendarez, age 18

The background music at Starbucks reminded me of New York. My first line came out so naturally, like the words were already born before I wrote them. I discovered that creativity is not so hard when you're telling the truth.

My mother is like New York with the lights turned off when she's sick. It's rare and depressing to see her sick, like it would be rare and depressing to see New York's lights off. She is like Casa Escobar when she's dressed up, hyped, and ready to dance. My mother is like her handy-dandy screwdriver — efficient yet needs to be recharged every now and then. She is like Christmas and Easter and May, loving and warm. She is like the portable, grey TV by her bed — always on, and always waiting. Hoping for the news to change.

My father is like his new, storm-grey Altima, stressed like his crashed, unfixed bumper. My sister is like a teddy bear or doll, with a heart that's easily wounded. My brother is like his backyard gigs — crazy, loud, and punk.

Julie is like the microwave, always in the kitchen. Tannia is like a Magic 8-Ball — you never know what you're gonna get. Katherine is talented and intelligent, just like a brand new iPod. She is like her garnet-colored shoes, tall and sophisticated, and always down-to-earth. Allison is like a pier at the beach at sunset — calm, strong, and wise.

My Sister Was Beautiful

Aisha Holden, age 16

My sister was beautiful. She would often spend hours in front of our long mirror pressing out her long Pocahontas-like hair and humming the song she and her boyfriend called theirs. Her eyes were bright and alive. When she smiled, she made everyone feel like smiling. Her smile was wide and showed off her perfect white teeth. She had super-long model legs, and she walked with pride.

Home

Portia J. Frazier, age 15

*My uncle is the most loving man I have ever met,
and I care about him very much. Whenever
I'm around him I really do feel home.*

Rotted teeth smirking their way into your heart.

The smell of Jack Daniels exhaled on

Laughing breath,

Dancing with the nicotine fragrance ever present in the air.

Warmth and beauty twinkling in his eyes

As all sorrow is left behind on the tides of his fifth drink.

Funny how I come back here, to work-roughened hands.

I am home.

This is part of a larger memoir, or perhaps a semi-autobiographical novel. I learned how important objects are in relation to memory.

Real Time

Elizabeth Gill, mentor

Back then a week was seven pancakes stacked with butter in between them and syrup drooling down layer after layer. That's why you ate them on Sunday so you could start all over again on Monday with a clean plate. Daddy poured them on the griddle in the middle of the stove where they would lava out into perfect rounds. When the bubbles popped, it was time to turn them over with the spatula. In its wooden handle, darkened with use and grease, two flat brass rivets secure the thin bent metal, narrow at the base and fanning out to no more than two inches at the top. When I heard that Jung had a favorite frying pan he used to talk to, I thought of my father's spatula that now resides in my kitchen drawer like an exile from the past. Every time I fold an omelet or flip a veggie-burger I feel my father's spirit tingle in my hand. Washing it and drying it with the focus of a Zen master, I often hold the timeworn steel to my lips, cool and smooth and more real than any mental memory of the man I lost too soon. Only a few pieces of that time and that place remain: four needlepoint chairs, some silver, some china, a few lace tablecloths, and the red glass collection, souvenirs of my early life given to me as my mother gradually sloughed off the material world in preparation for her death. Somehow I absorbed these artifacts into my already hopelessly cluttered house where I had lived for the past twenty years, and with them the shock that time had passed, that my parents had died, that both my daughters were now in college, that my husband and I were about to celebrate our silver wedding anniversary, and that the millennium I used to imagine as a child, wondering what it would be like to be as old as fifty-two, had come and gone. To see and even feel the persistence of a solid object through time, say, the original donut-shaped bottle of Shalimar Daddy had bought for Mother back in the 1930s (which I chipped the other day and didn't glue back together) is all I know of eternity.

One-legged Grandma

Fabiola Sandoval, mentor

We were called from over 1,200 miles away to care for my diabetic grandmother with an amputated leg. Shortly after settling into her bleak ranch, mama planted rose-bushes and fruit trees — orange, guava, and lemon. Gedeon and Jose, my brothers, were gardening, too. In no time the lifeless front yard blossomed alongside grandma's cries, mama's cooking, and children playing. My mother's resilience was manifested through the house's dry, dusty, and dirty yard giving way to life, through cobwebs cleared out, through scorpions chased away.

Grandmother spoke to the air calling for her deceased mama, brother, grandmother, and sister-in-law. In my twelve year-old mind, she was mingling with those on the other side. Her incoherent prayers to Los Espiritos Santos in between painful cries were her other one-sided conversations. The nights were filled with high-pitched aaghs and ughs. Awakened by her protests of pain and, some nights, from watching her hurting, and helpless to soothe her back to sleep, I would cry.

She died after Christmas day, and our mourning was appropriately filled with fiestas, posadas, firecrackers. Occasionally even my older brother, Jose, was able to take a break in the midst of death and join us.

We all shared the bedroom where she took her last breath. Her endless, habitual whimpers were gone. My mother was the one who changed her into clean clothing. Uncle Juvenal drove to town to buy the coffin. The men in our family carried it into the living room, and she was lifted from her bed and placed into the cream, crisp coffin.

As if a rooster cock-a-doodled the death of my grandmother, friends and family came swiftly to pay their respects, many leaving a Virgin Mary candle. Blue, red, white and green wax candles — some newly-lit, hot and cold, gooey — melted on the floor. The smell of death penetrated my nose, accompanied by soft sobs and the occasional wail from my mother. Some thirty guests drank coffee and stayed up through the warm night telling stories and praying. The men, who mixed their coffee with tequila, often burst into laughter. Under the star-bright sky illuminating the mourners in our tiny ranch, the laughter, cries, and prayers were my comfort.

Portly, Small, Large, Wide Honker

Hansanii Frazier Williams, age 14

Portly, small, large, wide honker

When she was young

She used to be regal

Now she's dour,

Adoring of things

That once were

Bitter-sweet and

Always glowering,

Her words are

Crisp and to the

Point, she never

Repeats a

Compliment twice,

Yet still generous.

Jean Valjean

Lovely Umayam, age 18

Renaissance man,
distorted into pieces of
cracked metal from the chains
of poverty and
rusty, rotting shackles of prison.

Jesus with a demonic fate,
treading on shallow, frothy mud,
left hand stealing bread, the right
kneading rosary beads on an
arthritic palm.

Fingers press onto corroding earth,
he swallows down the hour of death,
the soul surrenders,
like blood dripping onto the floor
of Toulon.

Oh, Renaissance man,
you let nineteen years slay you,
nineteen years pulsate on your hollow breast,
gagging from oppression,
your big almond-eyed innocence.

What became of you?
Your breath flies, flies away.
A face of a thousand stories,
wrinkled folds of skin, pores speaking, tracing
every miserable step of your journey.

But still, you give.
But still, you walk.

My Brother

Victoria Shao, age 18

Whizzing back and forth

From baseball practice, piano lessons, school

Singsong phrases punctuate quick, pounding beats of sneakered feet

Bounding onto my back and wriggling onto my head

(So much for a good hair day)

Then, just as quickly, he's gone again.

Off to something new.

My Mother

Ashtynn Baltimore, age 14

Fierce like a lion

Her walk, her talk, her attitude.

She speaks her mind.

Bold but soft.

Her eyes have a killer stare,

But show she's experienced hurt.

Her words spit fire, rocks,

Truth.

She's like a sister.

And no matter how random my feelings may be,

She always seems to make things O.K.

Assurance

Like chocolate.

Ode to My 16-Year-Old Revolutionary

Fielding Edlow, mentor

My mentee, Devon, and I decided to write a poem about each other. I thought back to when we were introduced on Match Day.

Devon and I met last of everyone
I waited and waited
I know how to wait
I'm good at it
People kept checking up on me
Don't worry, we have someone for you
Are you OK?
As if I wasn't OK
As if I suddenly developed a life-threatening aneurysm
The truth was, I didn't know if she would appear so
I continued to wait
Something I know how to do best in airports, in offices, wherever
And then I saw her

I saw me

The glasses refracting the hideous room lights
holding and illuminating all of us with our shiny noses,
open ears and disastrously split ends
There were nervous smiles exchanged and a permeating reassurance
that neither of us had been messed with in this particular circumstance
Even though
We both had been over and over and over again
When we both were somewhere between an embryo and an adult
I saw myself in her undercut hair, her swampy eyes, her walk,
the way she immediately scanned the room for problems, for issues

I am her

16 years ago and I go back there all the time

We are sisters in the broadest and gentlest term of the word
We are guarded, too smart for our own good and beautifully strung out individuals
who grew up way too fast,
and sometimes we ran straight into the sun and sometimes we ran right into the mud
which bunched our knees together and locked them in an incomprehensible design

this is my ode to my favorite revolutionary west of the Los Angeles River

Spoon My Heart

Jennifer Hoppe, mentor

My heart was found on some woman's driveway,
close-to-dead, stained by the streets,
gashed, finally scarred with
survival's signature.
I snatched my heart
from the glare
the traffic
the heat
so she could scamper around my house, outside my body,
ripping up kleenex,
barking at joggers she hasn't seen before.
I named my heart Spoon
a term of endearment from the 1930s
so says my thesaurus under "sweetheart."

My heart named Spoon packs in close to my knees,
moans when contentment cannot be contained.
My heart weighs twenty-six pounds,
with eyelash-long hair, black and white, smooth as flesh.
My heart smells like Fritos.

Napping, her breath catches up
and we exhale together,
snout to cheek.
Monkey eyes, human but encircled with fur,
open, lock with mine because
hearts need not use words.

Seeing St. Louis Win

Jayna Rust, mentor

I had one of those "a-ha" moments when I went to see the Cardinals/Padres game in San Diego. After I wrote this piece, my mentee, Melina, helped me edit it, and it was great hearing her prompt me the way I usually prompt her.

I came to PETCO Park hoping to see my St. Louis Cardinals win the division series, but once there, I couldn't help but love the energy of the San Diego supporters.

The two college-aged boys next to me had a sign that said "Cardinals ♥ Pooh Holes." Funny. The well-to-do guy to my left kept cursing at his home team in Spanish. Funny and passionate. But these fans' enthusiasm was nothing compared to the raucous young man two rows in front of me. He was often the only one out of his seat, pumping his arms high in the air when the Padres got an out. He belittled the Cardinals and he yelled for the Padres. Despite my love for the Cardinals, I couldn't help but admire him.

Sometime around the sixth inning, I noticed him retake his seat. His friend was gently pulling him along. Scooting past other spectators, my favorite fan looked up at the black sky, and I realized that he was blind.

I now watched him even more intently, but I began to question why he would waste his money on a game he couldn't even see. So, for a few plays I closed my eyes to imagine what it would be like to love baseball but not be able to see it. Without vision, I still knew when the Padres pitcher threw a strike. I knew when the ball was hit. And I could feel that the stadium was packed.

I slowly opened my eyes and thought of my clearest memories of sports — inevitably at the University of Missouri. I was immediately taken back to one of my favorites: the 100-plus degree day when my friends and I ran through the sprinklers and played on the beaten-up football field at Memorial Stadium. Then I remembered the first time I heard the student/alumni cheer of MIZ...ZOU. I had gotten chills for the whole two minutes the crowd yelled back and forth. Hearing the echoes of 60,000 fans chanting in unison for MIZZOU made me love the Tigers for life. I remembered the celebrations in the student section anytime any good MIZZOU thing happened at the Hearnes Center. Many times I was jumping up and down in the stands before falling onto another fan who would pick me up and give me an enthusiastic high-five. And I thought of the smell of Simmons Field as dew settled on the freshly cut grass before Friday night baseball games. Thinking of baseball, my mind finally wandered back to the Cardinals/Padres match-up in front of me. I looked once more at my favorite fan and I decided that even if I hadn't been able to see the Cardinals win, I still would have wanted to be there.

Leftovers

Cydney Neal, age 13

My cousins and I used to be in love with a group called B2K. My mom used to work with them, and once, after seeing one of their concerts, we were going to meet them. When the concert ended, we were super-ready. But ten minutes later, my mom told us, "I just heard that B2K can't see you guys because they have to go on tour, and they are leaving right now." Once we got in the car, my mom brought us some of B2K's leftovers. That was sort of gross so I just kept the fork. I ended up losing the fork, but the memory will last.

Surfboard

Rachel Wimberly, mentor

My mentee Julia, being a senior, was asked to lead part of the Poetry Workshop. She asked us to pick an object in our home and write, using free association. My surfboard keeps me somewhat sane in an insane world.

Surfboard

Alabaster white

Chaos

Tattoo

Total balance

Icy waters

Sea foam

Salt

Crushing force

Exhilaration

Tides

Breaks

Sand

Unwielding wetsuits

Fiberglass

Cracks

Sheer joy

Peace

Surfboard

Chapter 12 {Love}

Southeast of Venus

love love

Write what you know and what you don't know.

Passion
can fuel
brilliance.

When you love someone,
it's a great jumping off point for writing.

Our Eyes

Monika Zoltany, age 17

"Your eyes are so pretty," I said to you

A perfect pale green

Like moss drying out in the sun

Looking at all of me

Gentle and composed

And I feel soft

And desired.

"It's nothing to compliment me on," you said to me

"We have the same eyes."

I wasn't sure if that was true

So I looked in a mirror

And I saw my pretty pale green eyes looking back at me

Critical and indecisive

Looking at the world

Narrowed and suspicious.

And I think

I like our eyes better

When they are looking at me

Through you.

Curry Vindaloo

Deborah R. Bramwell, age 16

Curry Vindaloo is a rockstar

And you his best friend,

There for him

In broken-bottled anger

In painfully pure arousal.

He makes you weep.

He makes you gasp.

Paper's in the freezer —

Never again!

You swear —

You cry —

But he is a puppy

You've got no choice

But to take him back

Because you love every

Agonized

Breath.

And the Memories Still Linger

Julia Guest, age 17

I repeated the word "remember" in my mind for a while. Memories of a relationship I was in began to surface, and they all poured onto the page, one after the other.

I remember the day you called

A voice I hadn't heard since the fourth grade

I remember looking for your face among the crowd of teens —

Searching for an aged you

I remember digging our heels in the sand to dry our damp, salty feet

Making a figure of a sleeping man out of your hat and my towel

The thrill of running across the beach to refill the meter with change,

Knowing we'd left the ocean behind to baby-sit our belongings

Your hand wiping the sand off my boogie board

I remember my eyes pretending to scan the menu, but seeing nothing but your

face

The shy grin I gave you when you sang me your song

Your black chunky boot tapping to the beat of your melody

You said you didn't like pictures

You said it was because they didn't help you remember

We distanced

I remember when I was okay, but you weren't

When you were okay and I wasn't

Finding our picture and not remembering

Us

The Living Room

Steph Opitz, mentor

Our paint job is not finished; never will be.

The color is supposed to be classic — it is.

Covering our walls was a good test for our relationship.

My dad told me wallpapering is a good test for a relationship.

He said relationships need tests,

They are not linear.

We don't like wallpaper,

We used paint.

This relationship is sea foam,

It is sage.

His relationship was patterned, dated,

Hard to apply.

He should have used paint.

Lila

Denise Emanuel, mentor

At the Fiction Workshop, we talked about using both physical and non-physical ways of describing a character. I discovered that an entire story can develop from just one component, such as a bit of action, or a sense memory.

Please, God, Lila thought to herself, if you let me get away with this, I promise I'll never do it again. Her long dark hair had blown into one massive tangle. It blew out behind her, woven now into a bulky mass like the sleeve of a sweater or a winter scarf. She was holding onto Neil as tightly as she could, and although riding on the back of his big motorcycle had been thrilling just twenty minutes ago, it was an annoyance now. The noise, the dirt in the air, her tearing eyes and the way she knew it was making her mascara run were all getting on her nerves.

Neil swung the big bike into the driveway of the old Brightbach place. He slowed and the cycle bounced roughly over the rutted gravel. When he saw his brother Brian's Mustang nestled into the parking spot behind the two oak trees next to the back door, he came to a stop and revved the engine. As the motorcycle tilted to one side, supported only by Neil's black engineer-booted foot, he turned to Lila with a wounded look on his face.

"Why don't you just come over to my house tonight?" Lila asked, moving her hands ever so slightly along Neil's ribcage. "My parents will be out. And I've got to get back now anyway." Lila didn't have to utter another syllable. Neil spun the bike around and headed for town.

Neil dropped Lila at the far end of the park near the swimming pool. It was closed for the season, and the wall of the small cement block building that housed the snack bar provided good cover. Lila swung herself off the bike but lost her balance just long enough to come into contact with the motorcycle's shiny chrome exhaust pipe. The hot metal seared her skin, but Lila didn't even flinch. "Tonight," Neil said, as he zipped up his black jacket now that Lila's arms were no longer wrapped around him. Then he was gone.

Boys liked Lila, but she wasn't entirely sure why. Maybe it was her hair, the way it reached to her waist, the color of night in a town full of blonds. The blond girls were tall and thin, as a rule, like that English model Twiggy. Their legs reminded Lila of horses' legs, while her own legs reminded her of the Easter hams on display at Gerthner's Meat Market. She hoped that the burn on her calf wouldn't leave a scar.

Fantasy

Dominique Howard, mentor

I'd say I missed his touch, but that would imply I once experienced the pleasure

I'd say I missed his stare, but his eyes were always on another

It started in the back of my mind, but manifested to the front

It was all I thought about, dreamt about

I ate, slept, lived a fantasy

And loved every minute

Red Flags

Marna Bunger, mentor

He called at 5:15 p.m. on Valentine's Day to find out when I was going home. "I ordered flowers for you with guaranteed delivery. I don't want you to miss them."

They didn't come. They didn't come the next day. They didn't come the day after that, but that was the day I decided to release him from boyfriend duty permanently for other, non-flower-related reasons. His parting words were, "I still want to look into those flowers."

The following day, while I was cleaning my desk, I found my floral card and envelope from his prior delivery. He had said he ordered from the same florist for Valentine's Day. I called to check. An order had never been placed.

Honesty is a virtue in a town built on fantasies and lies. Until I find that guy, I'm going to keep my eyes wide open, pay attention to the red flags, and continue to date, I think.

After Dark

I love writing scenes for Lucas and Damian, characters from Angels in America. Damian is a passionate, almost fierce boy, determined to be a writer. Lucas is a quieter man who has yet to find his path.

Deborah R. Bramwell, age 16

The first time he read a poem, I thought he was talking about sex. That must sound harsh and judgmental. Perhaps it was — I was. He was sixteen and had written a poem called "Love Me" asking if someone loved him, describing his emotions as the person touched him. I assumed he meant romantic love as he perched on my bed in pajamas with hopeful, shimmering eyes, watching the page as he read. It sounded to me like a poem about sex, and that's how I responded. "It's really passionate," I said. "You really get the point across with connotation. It's different from most love poems."

Eventually Damian showed me the poems about his family. I recognized immediately the one he had shown me, and now, knowing its true meaning, I felt nauseous. This, my little contribution to his illness, the inability to read between the lines and know.

Years later, we were lying in his bed, curled together, and I stroked his chest over his heart and asked him, "Why don't you read me your poetry anymore?" He told me he no longer read poetry aloud. "Poems don't mean the same to everyone," he muttered, slightly breathless. "Everyone should take what they want."

I kissed him. "But you read me your prose," I protested. I don't know why I wanted him to read to me. It seemed romantic, and I was in the mood for romance.

"Prose is different. Prose has one distinct meaning."

"What if I wanted to read your poetry?"

"I would tell you they're under the bed, you can read as many as you like."

I sat on the edge of his bed with a stack of paperclipped papers. Some of them I had seen before, but most were new. And, honestly, some were crap. But for the most part these were much like Damian: honest, brutal, and thoroughly candid.

Wonder

Angela Martinez, age 18

Running around the wonder of my mind,
Looking around if you're the love of my life,
I just don't want to lose you.
I'm happy that I found somcone like you.

I don't want to lose you,
I want to keep you by my side.

I want to hold you.
I want to kiss you.
I want to love you.
I want to keep you.

Yeah, I want you.
Yeah, I need you.

I fell in love with you
On the first day we met

Yeah, I want you.
Yeah, I need you.

You are the spirit I've needed in my life.
You are the star I wish for.
You are the love of my life.
You are my everything.

I want to hold you.
I want to kiss you.
I want to love you.
I want to keep you.

Snoop

Melissa Anderson Sweazy, mentor

It wasn't tucked inside his journal, the one he keeps next to the bed with its smooth, innocuous cover. It wasn't the scraps of paper littered throughout the house that I know contain song lyrics, pieces of his scotch-taped heart that would sound like code if I had read them. This letter was on my computer, the one we've shared for weeks, the one that should have keys of diamonds and a mouse pad of gold judging by the way it is taken, cradled, possessed.

I shouldn't have read the letter. But it was just there — open, vulnerable, its intriguing title imploring the passerby to come and survey the feast. I read. I regretted it. Of course it's about her, the woman who forever ruined Europe for my love, who made Paris sound like a nasty word. It's the saddest song I've ever heard. And it's beautiful. When did he write this? I hear my husband in the kitchen washing dishes.

I'm helpless to stop myself. The floodgates open, and the monsters, that Girl, come tumbling out. I picture my husband wandering the streets of Paris, his heart slipping through his fingers. My husband's blank face and bloody fingers staring up at Parisians from the front page of Le Monde, headlines screaming "Qu'est arrivé au coeur de son homme?"

He's playing chess alone in a café in the Marais. His cigarette smoke curls into a heart-eating dragon in the chill of an autumn night. At this café he was not my husband. Here he was madly in love with a woman whose mouth reminds him of eating peaches over a sink in July.

Date stamp. The letter was written eight years ago. Relief. The woman is a hazy figment, a wraith with babies and housework and memories. I wrap my arms around my husband's waist as he finishes the dishes. His heart beats.

The Constant Routine

Margaret Padilla, age 14

I am obsessively in love.
My mind is in the sky
daydreams are constant routine
the earth revolves around his image.
Everybody feels that her love is unique,
even Mrs. Evans.
Her rambling could cause anyone to fall asleep.
She's too old for modern love.
Even Robin.
Her Valley Girl dialect is foreign to romance.
She talks more than she thinks,
she shops more than she prays.
Even William.
His wannabe gangster-technique
would make the Pope laugh,
he has no brain for truth.
I'm guilty of over-analyzing
simple comments and words.
I don't trust others easily.
Yet if I can love
maybe they can too.

I was inspired to write this poem by songs that my iPod played on shuffle.

Metros & Buses

Lilah Khoja, age 15

I said, I'm tired,

And I don't know anymore

I wish I could hold you, you said.

I'm scared, I cried, I'm scared.

And you, you were on my shoulder

And you shifted slightly,

As if you heard me and

You, I love you.

I whispered, I'm lost

I'm lost I said. And all

The houses we passed by

Seemed to cry and all

The trees we passed by seemed the

Same and you, I love you.

love

216

Nevermind

Baetoni-Milo Walker, age 15

When we meet I want fire in my eyes,
When I kiss you I want it to be passionate,
I won't cry if you leave me now,
I won't live and will die slowly.

Why must I be like the devil's disguise?
Dressed up in a suit,
Trying to look like everyone else,
Committing crimes,
Deceiving others into thinking I'm someone else,
Lying and murdering.

But when I kiss you none of that makes sense,
So I'll give up my ways and just dress in jeans.

Don't Leave Me Hanging

Julia Guest, age 17

INT. HIGH SCHOOL AUDITORIUM
BACKSTAGE - DAY

SAM, shy and mysterious, plays
the guitar. SARA, the girl he
has a crush on, approaches.

SAM
Tonight is going to rock, Sara.
I'm psyched that you're coming
to our show.

Sara is quiet. She looks down,
seeming annoyed.

SARA
Yeah . . . it should be a good
time.

SAM
You're going to get to meet my
whole family, Sara. They're all
so excited. Let's just hope
they don't flake on me again.

SARA
Sam –

Sam cuts her off, speaking
rapidly.

SAM
They do it time and time
again. Always leaving me
hanging. This is the one time
they actually said the words,
"We'll be there."

Sara waits for Sam to finish.
Her expression is serious.

SARA
Sam, why didn't you tell me
you don't have a home?

Sam is shocked.

SAM
What? What do you mean? I . . .

SARA
Charlie told me that you ran
away two years ago. You live
on and off with your uncle's
friend. He said you don't
always have a place to go at
night.

Sam scoffs.

SAM
Sara, I wouldn't lie to you.

SARA
You've made up an entire life
of lies. The three younger
sisters? The dog named Benny,
the big house, where your
perfect family lives?

Sam turns away, shaking his
head in denial.

SAM
What are you saying? You
think I'm . . . homeless?
Well, I'm not. Look, if
you don't want to come to
the concert, that's fine.
I'm meeting the rest of
the band outside in a
minute . . .

SARA
Sam, I don't want to abandon
you. Can we just talk about
this? I still – I still want
to know you, no matter what
the truth is.

Sam regards Sara. He smiles
slowly and shakes his head,
disagreeing.

SAM
Don't kid yourself. You're
right, I have nothing. I don't
have a house, no sisters, no
parents. I don't eat meals
around the table with my
family. I have nothing.
Nothing to give you.

SARA
You have the truth.

SAM
The truth?

Sara approaches Sam and
gently places her hand on
his shoulder.

SARA
The truth.

Flight 416

Lovely Umayam, age 18

Wednesday morning and my mind is fast asleep
Succumbing to the numbness of nothing
Left to inhale
Ancient airline rugs
Engraved with footprints of
Travelers unknown
Hushed up, mouths plastered by
Oxygen masks keeping
Their secrets inside

I, too, have a secret to keep
A hidden wound, numb and profound
Guiltlessly growing
A romantic bliss trapped within
The ancient art form
Of creases and folds
Of paper airplanes
Propelled, plunging
Limp on the ground

I, too, have a secret to tell
Love for a boy who may not love me back
A fear heavier
Than all the metal and steel
Wings too weighted and worn to fly
I, too, feel the heaviness
The ancient whisper of the winds
Carrying dead weight
On my shoulders

With no books and a broken iPod
I keep silent
Embracing turbulence
Listening to the electronic humdrum
Left in peace
Using the cocktail cart
To drink away
A love crisis
34,000 feet below

Reveal more,

Dive into that,

Chapter 13 {Writer's Block}

To get past Writer's Block, turn to Chapter 14 →

Chapter 14 {Experiments}

I am a used tissue. I am cold
and moist, and my owner should
have thrown me away hours ago.
How I wish I was at the bottom of
a trashcan, drying out and living out
the last moments of my disgusting
existence.

Reach your hand in your pocket or
purse. What did you find? Where did
you get it? What does it remind you of?
Tell the story from the object's point of
view!

Uncover and Discover:

Writing Experiments from WriteGirl

Write upside down, across two pages, follow the border. Write in a spiral.

Create a Dedication Page and dedicate your journal to someone or someplace you love or someplace you love

Crack the Cover!

Write a Warning to ward prying

Write with markers, crayons, paintbrushes, or charcoal.

Pretend your journal is a door wormhole where would if time glue to

Tape or include photographs, ticket stubs, wrapper Chinese fortunes and other ephemera.

Cut or fold pages, create windows, use paint or dye edges.

stain with coffee, store chewing gum make a rubbing of a c press rosemary branch

Crack the Cover, Write & Play, the WriteGirl Way!

Write upside down, across two pages, follow the border, write in a spiral.

Create a Dedication Page and dedicate your journal to someone or something or somewhere you love.

Write a Warning Page — sort of like a Guard Dog for your journal.

Pretend your journal is a door, a wormhole, a time machine...where would it take you?

Tape or glue photographs, ticket stubs, wrappers, Chinese fortunes and other ephemera.

Stain pages with coffee, store your chewing gum, squish bugs, make a rubbing of a coin, press rosemary branches.

Cut or fold pages, create windows, dye edges, rip corners.

Write with markers, crayons, paintbrushes, charcoal.

experiments

227

I had fun with this piece and, clearly, I have many questions.

Warning

Keren Taylor, mentor

Warning: Do not read any further. What do you want from reading my journal? The insides of me? My secret thoughts? My secrets? Will it make you want to write down your own free-fall rant? Do you keep a journal? Did you ever? Where is it now? In a shoebox, in a dresser, at the back of a metal filing cabinet? Do you feel like the same person? Was it all about the one who didn't love you back and how your mother made you so mad? Do you wonder how people would react if they came across it, read parts of it, perhaps even finding a reference to themselves? Did you write about hating yourself and wanting to change, but not knowing how? Did you write letters to people, knowing you would never send them? Did you write lists of places you wanted to go, things you wanted to do? Did you fill every page, single-spaced, with fast, curvy writing, angled to the right? Did you just stop one day, before the journal was full, and never open it again, except one day, after college when you were cleaning and accidentally found it with its lined pages all stiff and crisp? Did you flip to somewhere in the middle and read for a while, standing up, breathing shallow, trying to imagine who you were when you wrote all of that? Are you embarrassed by some of what you wrote, your cravings, your obsessions, your pain? Do you see patterns that are familiar to who you are now? Do you think people are inherently good? Do you think if someone wants everyone to like her, that she is insecure, starved for something, or just narcissistic? Did you have a good relationship with your father? Did you ever write about it? How did things turn out for you, so far? Did you reach your goals, find love, make money, succeed at something? Warning: This is my personal journal. If you are still reading this, please stop now.

Use every sense and eat cookies while you write.

Be Afraid. Be Very Afraid

Tracy Chait, mentor

Death by journal awaits inside this cover! I mean it!!! I don't use exclamation points like that every day, you know. But seriously. Anyone who's ever dared to venture past Page One hasn't made it any further. I don't really want to get into all the details. The things that have happened. But they weren't pretty. If people just listened to directions, I wouldn't have had to do the things I've done. I wouldn't need all that rope in the back of my car, the duct tape, those heavy instruction manuals with titles like, Maiming for Dummies, or How to Nab a Burglar. Gosh, they've been taking up valuable bookshelf space. And who doesn't need room for more journals?

Inspiration comes with practice.

Warning

Laura Hurtado, age 16

WARNING:
This Is an Official Warning

Do not turn another page of this journal if you have no wish to read the rambling accounts of a teenage girl, her mindless drawings, and other such things. Do not turn another page if you are not one who enjoys having a good time, hanging out with friends, and spending time with family. Do not turn another page if you are not one who lives life to its fullest and loves it to death. So just remember, you have been forewarned.

...mily. Do not turn another page if you are not one who lives life to its fullest and loves it to death. So just remember you have been forwarned.

Laura Hurtado

Dedication Page

Melissa Castillo, age 15

I am inspired by my mom even though she'll never know it. I am inspired by the hope she has, by her will to forgive and how she has overcome so much. I am inspired by so many things she does. I hope to one day have that inner strength that is silent but so powerful.

Select a page in a book or magazine and copy every fourth word. Write a poem using those words.

WhereWouldIt Take You?

This piece grew out of the first workshop where we received our new journals. We were asked to imagine them as doors and write where they would lead.

Lena Brooks, age 17

Seriously, am I supposed to know where it would go?

I get on the bus, and I do not know where the bus goes. I hate direction because I really don't understand direction. It's cool, I just move. I'm displaced. What's to lose in a century of displacement? Like generation diaspora or whatever. Can't commit to my own worlds right now, can't commit to my own placement. Whatever. Warm in the car. I let my eyes go glassy, glassy. Let my eyes go glassed over. Fish and lizard eyelids pulled all down the balls. You know I can see everything like a fish can while he sleeps. Me in my fishbowl car on the wide road. Water warm. We take the 5, we take the 2, we take the Glendale freeway. On the overpass I don't breathe, on the underpass I don't breathe either. Match my eyes to my skin to my scales, forget the air and let the gills sprout up. Don't need to breathe, just need to need. Comfortable in a soft car, cross the street and I'm well bound by the double yellow line, my own warm clothes. Watch the skyline and the pavement rose, roses. On soft mornings, fat cheek of sky and you can't feel the bones. You just know the bones are there making waking bodies, raising suns over satellite nights.

Lucky 7
Word Lotto

Ask a friend to write down seven random words of any variety —
nouns, verbs, adjectives, numbers, colors, anything! The more unusual the
word, the better. Then write a poem using these seven words. Write it fast,
Trust the associations that you make.

TIP:
Pay attention to your line breaks. How does your poem look on the page?
Is it long and skinny or does it look more like a paragraph?

CHALLENGE:
Build the poem around a specific theme.

Show & Tell

Allie List, age 15

7 words:

pop,
duplicitous,
lame,
spider,
heartthrob,
flabbergasted,
fame

Open-mouthed, she faces the heartthrob,

Flabbergasted at his pop fame.

Sad thing is, she's more stunning than he ever was.

He sees this,

He's all over her, a spider.

She hands him her phone number

A lame, hopeful smile paints her face

Not realizing his meaning in this is duplicitous.

But then, so is hers.

She just won at Show and Tell.

Write the worst poem you can possibly write. Use clichés, pretentious words, and beat your readers over the head with your point. Felt good, didn't it? Now get back to work. The point is, don't be afraid to write a bad poem. If it takes a hundred bad poems before you can produce a poem you like, fine, get that hundred out of the way.

Blue Plus Red Equals Purple

Stephanie Lopez, age 17

3 words:
Tokyo, rapper,
guru

The violence, the drugs, the shouts of, "Where you from?" did not appeal to Lil' Guru anymore. The bloodshed from wearing the wrong color had left his hands filthy and his eyes blind. The music and gunshots had left him deaf. The rapper had lost everything he had earned. Lil' Guru could no longer hear any beats no matter how loud he beat boxed. He jumped up in the air and slammed his feet onto the ground of Downtown Tokyo. He jumped again till he felt as if knives were stabbing at his feet. He yelled and then cried, for he had heard himself. He continued to stamp his feet and eventually let his fingers snap beats that seemed to scream in his ear. Lil' Guru stomped beats and began to rap. He could speak again! Colors of Blue swarmed past him, but he did not care. He had found the love that he had lost.

Terra Cotta

Cydney Neal, age 13

7 words:
blazing,
terra cotta,
glitter,
beads,
spit,
protest,
drenched.

The blazing hot tortilla came home with me

In a spit-covered terra cotta pot.

The sizzling sound makes me

Realize how it is drenched in boiling oil.

The blazing hot heat hits my face

When opening the beautifully decorated terra cotta pot.

The paint here, glitter there,

Beautiful beads surround the whole thing.

The blazing hot tortilla came home with me

In a spit-covered terra cotta pot.

The market complains that I stole the tortillas

Even though I protest.

Family Celebration

Lexa Houska, mentor

7 words:
Jack Daniels,
Jesus Christ,
gargantuan,
hummingbird,
owl,
snow,
communion.

The special day is gargantuan

A communion of anger, Jack Daniels and Jesus Christ,

overwhelmed.

Outside, the day furthest from summer

when tears weep from the eaves

and freeze into sharp spears that ting the window

Still with desperation, elegant with sadness.

They are dazzled by lights that flicker and sizzle

and buzz like a hummingbird,

exhausted.

A new day hoots like an owl,

breathing deeply, promising

that night will fall

with a blanket of dissolving snow.

Follow your fear.
Don't back away from subjects that make you
uncomfortable, and don't try to keep your personal
demons off the page. Even if you never publish the
writing, you have to push yourself and write as
honestly as possible.

My Pet Monkey Nachos

Laura Hurtado, age 16

7 words:
serendipity,
chimes,
monkey,
phosphorescent,
subterranean,
nachos,
Kansas.

Me and my pet monkey Nachos,
Oh, such phosphorescent friends!
A tornado took us away from Kansas —
Lions! Tigers! Subterranean chimes! Oh my!
Serendipity sury, Serendipity surrah,
Serendipity sury,
Oh, what a wonderful time!

Wandering through the sea of poppies,
Hallucinations galore.
I thought I saw a purple man,
But Nacho said it wasn't so.
Closer, closer we came
Until —
Run, Run as fast as you can
It can catch us
For it's the gingerbread man!

Running, Running as fast as we can,
Me and my pet monkey Nachos
Oh thank butterscotch!
We've found a safe haven!

What's this?
Oh dear, dear me.
It so appears
That me and my pet monkey Nachos
Have stumbled into
Mr. Purple People- and Monkey-Eater's house!

The Collective Quiet

Rachel Wimberly, mentor

7 words:
zany,
hobbled,
prickly,
dubious,
puncture,
zealous,
drenched.

My family is not zany.

They are too hobbled with Puritan pride

To be something so prickly.

My mother, calm, cool, collected,

Is dubious of anything that might puncture

The zealous protection of her veneer of sanity.

Fighting it, I am often drenched in frustration.

experiments

Practice using as few words as possible.

Pink Slip

Color is all around us and can inspire us to write.
Hardware stores have paint chips, and printing companies give
out samples of colored paper. At the WriteGirl Poetry Workshop, we asked
everyone to pick a different colored slip of paper from a box and dive
into the color to see what happened. What do you associate with this
color? What does this color make you feel? What are all the things that
are this color? If you were this color, what kind of person would you be?
If this color spoke to you, what would it say?

Brown

Marylou Raygoza, age 14

Brown. It gives me a warm, hollow feeling. It reminds me of my small barn house back in Long Beach. I lived there for nine years. I hated that house, but once we had to move, I really missed it.

The house was made of wood. It was the color of my lawn. (Obviously, we didn't take care of it.) It was the color of my neighbors. It was the color of the carpet where I spent many hours watching TV.

Brown reminds me of the things I left behind. When someone says the word brown I get happy and think of my small barn house in Long Beach. Then I think of lots of people I let down. I don't know why.

A Slice of Sky

Shauna Smith, mentor

a slice of sky

not quite clear

moving mountains of marbled grey

clouds that tower

to the edge of the atmosphere

what are they hiding?

shadows across the city

light and dark exchange space

clouds slip over glossy high-rises,

alleyways, downtown intersections

light and dark move along

switch the checkerboard colors

across the city grid.

Sixty-Pound Paper

Pamela Turski, mentor

But cosmic orange 60# might carry more weight. It must,

this rebel hue on the spectrum's fringe.

The color of chaos,

torn from the sun

an orange as bold as rage

as bright as truth.

When nothing is coming, start writing very fast — any word, phrase or sentence that comes to mind. Do that for about a minute, then go back to your piece. (This is called flushing.) Whether you use anything you flushed is up to you. You can, but that's not the purpose.

Cosmic Orange

Michele Summers Colon, mentor

Cosmic orange feels silly

I have cargo pants this color

When I wear them

I feel clown-like

This color found me today

To remind me

To play

Like my child

Cosmic orange is cool

Like me

Like her

Fun and playing go together well

Like my daughter and me

The message is "have fun and play"

Like a child

Like my child

Like me

Pick a color and write about it.

Paper Stock

Kristin Holloway, mentor

I am Fox River

At first glance, drab, dreary, dry

Look again

Complex, textured, flecked with blue

Silver is my foundation

A fancy kind of grey

Grey as noise is

Sound pound to the ground

Sound pound to the ground

But let's call it silver

Silver let's name it

Repeat again and make it true

I, Fox River, am fancy and silver

And proud to be flecked with blue

Blushing is a wonderful thing, and I'm going to stop hiding it.

The Color of Blush

Catherine Cook, mentor

The color of blush

hiding under my skin

my white-freckled skin

a blanket

soft, subtle, and safe

drenched and protected

in my mortal comfort zone.

Almost suffocating

sometimes,

the stale surface.

But I can't be safe forever.

I must learn to blush,

to live and blush

be scared and blush,

because I need to be discovered.

I need to be found,

I cannot hide forever.

I will blush until my skin becomes a permanent blush

and I am found out for good,

uncovered, exposed.

No more fear, no holding back.

This Paper

Karen Toledo, age 13

The color is special to me

I don't know its name, but I'd name it Dull.

When I feel it, it feels dull.

If my life were it, it would be dull.

Dullness does dance,

Dullness can be dull.

Dullness can be only ordinary.

Dullness could be like everyone.

Dullness will be dull.

If I sent this to someone,

I'd leave it blank and leave

The person to figure it out

Because its name is dull.

Love your characters as much as yourself.

Piece of Paper

Ariel Edwards-Levy, age 16

It's the color of my old bedroom walls

And smells like my father's old office

And so, lest you get nostalgic, I realized

and he relocated by choice

Lest you get nostalgic

My old walls were dirty, like apathy, old stucco,

Far more nursing home than nursery

Lest you get nostalgic

My father drove two hours to work each

Morning and back in rush hour each night

Pink Ice - a Frankenstein of a name

Created by the same mad marketer who gave us

Blue Raspberry

Lest you get nostalgic, lest you weep for the past,

Lest you deign to care

Help: I'm trapped in a paint chip and apathy factory.

Ariel Edmonstery ~~Eooothi~~ fails an attempt at poetry

Piece of paper

It's the color of my old bedroom
walls, and smells like my father's old office-
and so lest you get nostalgic, I repainted and he relocated
    by choice.
Lest you get nostalgic,
my old walls were dirty, ~~all~~ like apathy, old stucco,
        ~~clad~~ far more nursing home than nursery.
    Lest you get nostalgic
my father drove two hours to work each ~~way~~
~~in~~ morning ~~and~~ back in rush hour each night.
    Pink ice—~~unless that's~~ ~~by~~ Frankenstein of a name
created by the same mad marketer who gave us
        Blue Raspberry.
Lest you get nostalgic, lest you ~~yearn~~ for the past,
    lest you ~~deign~~ deign to care.
    Help: I'm trapped in a paint chip and apathy factory.

Around the House

Your home is rich with objects that reflect your identity, your travels, your culture, your past. Choose an object in your home and write about all that it represents. Where did it come from? How long have you had it? Where do you keep it and why? What do others think about it?

TIP:
It helps to look at the physical object as you write.
If you can, hold it in your hand.
Notice temperature, textures, weight, small details.

Tablecloth

Alejandra Cardenas, age 13

Kept in a plastic bag in the garage

To keep it clean

So much love in each stitch

Handmade, future family heirloom-to-be

passed on to me

Wrinkled, crinkled hands were shaking

Out of joy or age, I don't know,

As she handed it to my mother

We left, and I know she cried

Great-grandmother

I will love you forever

I discovered that I was right about the dusty old Virgin Mary upon my shelf.

The Virgin Mary

Devon Regina DeSalvo, age 16

An old remnant of a religious past

Nobody really pays her any mind

She sits high upon her dusty shelf

A knick-knack

A dusty old trinket

That is all she has become

Once held in great esteem

Now she watches over us

From her high shelf

We pay her no mind

Tupperware

Laura Hurtado, age 16

Plastic Tupperware container (round and size large).

Sunbathes in the microwave.

Parties with soups from around the world.

You sleep in a bed,

It has sleepovers every night in the cabinet under the stovetop.

You take a shower in the tub,

It takes a bath in the dishwasher.

You may hate getting shots,

It hates getting forked or spooned!

Don't forget it in the back of the fridge, full of moldy leftovers!

Please contact if lid found.

Multiply by five.

Try going 5-D with your writing —
use smell, touch, sound, sight, and taste.
Use each of your senses to describe something, somewhere,
or someone. Got a sixth sense? Use that, too!

Flavors

Carol A. Forbes, mentor

Ackee and salt fish with fried dumplings.

My father's hands knead the dough and

drop them in the crackling skillet.

My mother's slender fingers chop the onions and toss them into the pan.

Scotch bonnet peppers set the mix ablaze.

They dance together, releasing their flavors and become one.

Fried plantains add sweetness.

Blue Mountain coffee summons the royal touch.

Chocolate tea for the children.

Laughter, stories told, prayers said around the kitchen table.

Memories of the home we left behind and grateful for the home we have now.

My Daughter in 5 Senses

Stephanie Allen, mentor

Navy blue eyes pooled

in whites bright

as firecrackers

when every day is new

opportunity to sing

her Walt Whitman declaration

dance trance rhythms

interrupted by belly laughs

or gut sobs

Mid-20s emotions

tangled round her

own throat

Got to break free

like Houdini

Hands too small to grab

the chunk of the world

she deserves

I nestle her head

in my lap

and stroke the honey silk

breathe her chamomile and musk

Keep a dream journal.
Dreams are your mind at it's most creative.
Listen to them. Don't feel you have to write
about your dreams. If you want to, fine, but
the main goal is to see what thoughts the
dreams lead you to.

Don't love your characters too much —
the story will be no good if the characters never suffer.

Chapter 15 {WriteGirl Defined}

very time we meet. We always have things t

I have to know myself so that I can know the world. Inspira

ing. Don't stop. Write with a friend. Write alone by a green

tones, marking the weather today. Now is the right time. Wh

bit. Breathe and write. Write often. **Write what you want**

e me to another world on the page. I love being surprised by

es from. I write because I want to say something b

something is, it is simply an urge to put forth some s

read and take away, or not. **Through writing I understand**

more interested in writing more personal, first-person short stories. Go deep

ite because I am scared of it and when I'm scared of somet

make the changes.

ee what it has to tell me. What am I scared of knowing?

bit more every time we meet. We always have things to write about

I write to get to what is good and brave and strong inside me. I wr

st keep writing. Don't stop. Write with a friend. Write alone by a green lake. **Wh**

age, like hailstones, marking the weather today. Now is the right time. What do you

slow down a bit. Breathe and write. Write often. **Write what you want to know.** What thing

my mind take me to another world on the page. I love being surprised by what I write a

where it comes from. I write because I want to say something but am not

re what that something is, it is simply an urge to put forth some small or large

yself, to put it out there in the world, and know that I have put it there for

anyone, to read and take away, or not. **Through writing I understand my largest an**

oughts. I write because I am scared of it and when I'm scared of something I come ba

nd over, to see what it has to tell me. What am I scared of knowing? What am I

thinking? I write to get to what is good and brave and strong inside me. I write because th

life I know and I want to experience it deeply. **The hardest thing to do is jus**

ur desk and write. When things are terrible, write. When things are great, w

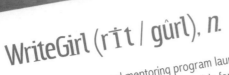

WriteGirl (rīt / gûrl), n.

1. A creative writing and mentoring program launched in 2001 that pairs professional women writers with teen girls for one-on-one weekly mentoring, monthly creative writing workshops and public readings in Los Angeles.

2. A nine-month season of writing, sharing, inspiration, and discovery, culminating with the publication of an anthology of work from all members (girls and women).

3. A bold female writer with something to say.

Positive energy, attitude-free people.

I met people who made me laugh and made me think.

Today made me rem
started writing

tively, we're working to make a difference in the life a girl and to empower ourselves in the process.

writegirl

TARGAD 2/18/06

I LOVED THE SOUND OF SILENCE OF 120 GIRLS WOMEN IN 1 ROOM, BROKEN ONLY BY THE RUSTLING OF PAPER & CLICKING OF PENS. HEADS BOWED & BROWS FURROWED IN THE FOCUS OF WRITING TOGETHER, YET INDIVIDUALLY.

Every month I come here
to give of my time.
And every month I leave here,
certain I got more than I gave.

energy
paper rustling
chatting
small groups gathering
women
girls
writing
books
wide eyes
smiling eyes
laptops clicking
chewed-up pens
new friends
old friends
silence of minds writing
bold choices
soft-spoken
shy girls
loud girls

many girls
calm women
tall women
wise women
hilarious women
focus
brilliance

Mentor (men/tôr), n.f., v.

n. 1. A wise and trusted counselor or teacher.

2. A professional female writer in Los Angeles dedicated to empowering the next generation of young women writers.

v. 1. To advise, master and guide.

2. To meet weekly, armed with a journal and a pen, with a teen girl (SEE Mentee) at a cool writing spot (a local café, a library, etc.), to create literary magic.

We trade secrets. She has been a bit boy crazy lately.

Words
Observation
Crushes
Excitement
Surprise

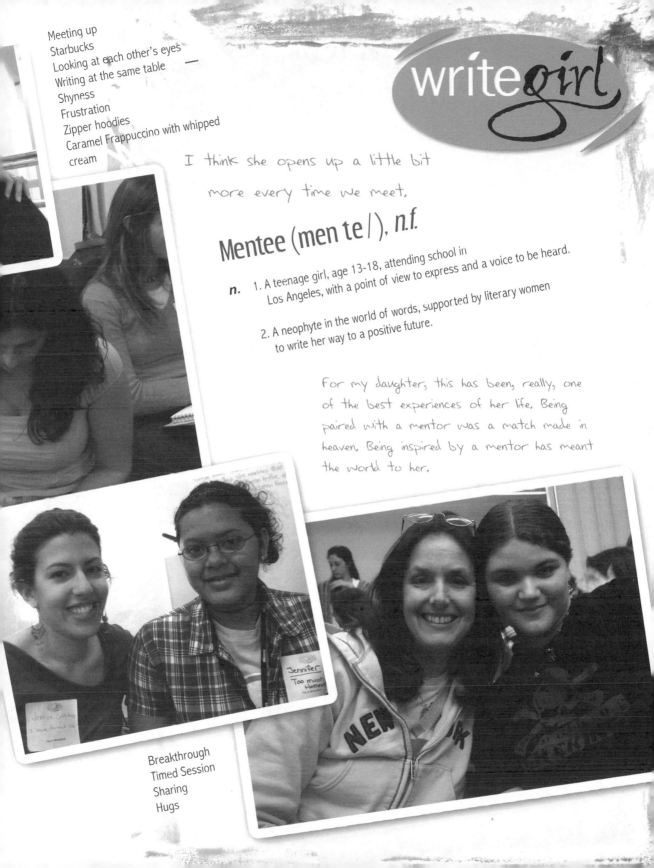

Meeting up
Starbucks
Looking at each other's eyes
Writing at the same table
Shyness
Frustration
Zipper hoodies
Caramel Frappuccino with whipped
cream

writegirl

I think she opens up a little bit
more every time we meet.

Mentee (men te /), n.f.

n. 1. A teenage girl, age 13-18, attending school in
Los Angeles, with a point of view to express and a voice to be heard.

2. A neophyte in the world of words, supported by literary women
to write her way to a positive future.

For my daughter, this has been, really, one
of the best experiences of her life. Being
paired with a mentor was a match made in
heaven. Being inspired by a mentor has meant
the world to her.

Breakthrough
Timed Session
Sharing
Hugs

Workshop (wûrk / shop/), n.f.

n.

1. A monthly gathering of teen girls and professional women writers at the Yucca Community Center in Hollywood, CA, to discover, empower, experiment and transform through various forms and styles of writing.

2. A creative congregation of over 50 volunteers and over 50 mentoring pairs, exploring such writing genres as fiction, poetry, journalism, songwriting, character and dialogue and creative nonfiction.

3. An energetic exchange of ideas and advice all day long on Saturdays, including a lunch worth writing about.

Trying
Creative
Challenging
Ready
Insight
New forms, styles, approaches
Discovering myself
Pulling it out of me
All in it together
Courage

Today I learned to stretch myself — my thoughts.
There is more than one way to say something.

Energy
Openness
Entertaining
Foud
 Learning
Experimenting
Sharing
Laughing
Taking chances

writegirl

THINK ABOUT
A SPACE YOU
FEEL COMFORTABLE IN.
① Tell a close friend what's
   so great about it.
② Tell your parents what's
   so great about it.

...e talent in this room brought me to my knees,

Publication (pub / li k a / shen), *n.f.*

n. 1. An annual anthology of writing from women and girls created during a nine-month season of creative gatherings and mentoring meetings.

2. The intimate expressions, inner thoughts, observations, insights, imaginative musings and dreams captured in language and arranged between the front and back cover.

3. An explosive and revealing tome notorious for inspiring the young and the old, women and men alike, to write out loud.

WriteGirls write truth, and it is stranger than fiction.

I have seen the birth of
tomorrow's screenwriters,

Wisdom told by all ages,

So many colors, different faces and beautiful minds,

Deadlines
Word count
Release
Submissions
Compilation
Meaning
Dynamic
Deep

Exposed
Name in print
Professional
Impressive
Proud

The world is wide inside these girls,

I was cranky and had a headache and all this positive energy made me feel better.

Performance,

n. 1. The oral expression of the written word offered in a bookstore, café, or book fair, for the purpose of overcoming the fear of public speaking, gaining confidence and sharing one's writing and ideas with the community.

2. A monthly opportunity to reveal oneself through the written word, in front of a live audience, frequently associated with such side effects as butterflies in the stomach, "mic fright," perspiration, shaky hands, rapid pulse, and a thrilling sense of self and accomplishment.

Poised, talented, courageous, beautiful. The girls who read today rocked my world.

When the girls read aloud, I am
so proud of the risks they take
to let others in that I am
moved to tears.

write girl

Speaking Out
Listening
Laughter
Community
Putting it out there
Applause
Crowds
MC
Backstage
Standing Tall

d that I read aloud

e not knowing what
I leave here wanting
part of it.

Leadership: The WriteGirl "Engine"

Executive Director:	**Keren Taylor**
Associate Director:	**Allison Deegan**
Program Coordinator:	**Phoebe Brauer**
Website, Branding, Book Design:	**Sara Apelkvist**
Graphics (Invitations, flyers):	**Wendy Tigerman**
Workshop Curriculum:	**Kimberly Minten Purcell**
Event Planning:	**Steph Opitz, Erica Blodgett**
Event Support:	**Maia Akiva, Dominique Howard**
Fundraising:	**Kelly Merryman, Tracy Chait, Katy Melody**
Public Relations:	**Rachel Wimberly, Sarah Leonard, Colleen Sharkey**
Mentoring Managers:	**Marlys West, Jennifer Hoppe**
Mentee Communications:	**Ashley Wilson**
Publications:	**Erica Kelly**
Book Publicity and Sales:	**Elizabeth Gill**

WriteGirl Advisory Board

Barbara Abercrombie, Novelist, UCLA Writing Instructor, Lecturer

Shelley Berger, Poet and Beyond Baroque Poetry Teacher

Mark Bisgeier, Entertainment Attorney

Suzie Coelho, Lifestyle Expert, Author and HGTV Television Host

Mark Cull, Red Hen Press Publisher & Co-Founder

Allison Deegan, Marketing Consultant, Screenwriter

Kai EL´ Zabar, Writer, Editor, Multimedia Consultant

Elizabeth Forsythe Hailey, Novelist

Mollie Gregory, Author, Teacher, Writing Consultant

John Marshall, Vice President-Manufacturing, RR Donnelley

Vickie Nam, Writer, Editor of *Yell-Oh Girls* (Asian-American teen anthology), Interactive Producer

Maria del Pilar O'Cadiz, Ph.D., Executive Director & Research Specialist: Collaborative After School Project, California Department of Education

Joy Picus, Former Los Angeles City Council Member, Community Organizer

Cecilia Rasmussen, Writer and Columnist for the *Los Angeles Times*

Deborah Reber, Author

Aleida Rodríguez, Poet, Editor, Educator, Translator, Publisher

Diane Siegel, Museum, Library and Education Consultant, Community Organizer

Keren Taylor, Songwriter, Poet, Visual Artist
(Founder and WriteGirl Executive Director)

Community Connections

Participating Schools:

Artesia High School
Belmont High School
Birmingham High School
Calabasas High School
Camino Nuevo Middle School
Centennial High School
Claremont High School
Cleveland High School
Crossroads School
Destiny Academy
Eagle Rock High School
Fairfax High School
Fremont High School
Gardena High School
Glendale High School
Gompers Middle School
Hamilton High School
Harvard Westlake School
High Tech High School
Immaculate Heart High School
Irving Middle School
John Adams Middle School
John Burroughs Middle School
John Marshall High School
Junipero Serra High School
L.A. Academy Middle School
La Cañada High School
LACES High School
Las Flores Middle School
Le Lycée Français de Los Angeles
Los Angeles High School
Marlborough School
Metropolitan High School

Nia Educational Charter School
North Hollywood High School
Our Mother of Good Council Middle School
Pacific Hills High School
Palisades Charter High School
Palms Middle School
Portola Middle School
San Pedro High School
Santa Monica High School
South Pasadena High School
St. Bernard's High School
St. Margaret's Episcopal School
St. Paul High School
Thomas Star King Middle School
Torrance High School
West Valley Christian School

Referring Organizations:

Bresee Community Center
Mentor LA
Los Angeles Times
Para Los Niños
Poets & Writers Magazine
Step Up Women's Network
UCLA Extension Writers Program
VolunteerMatch
Writers Guild of America, west
Writers Guild of America Foundation
Yucca Community Center

WriteGirl Supporters

WriteGirl would like to thank the following for their generous support:

Foundations and Corporations

Adams Family Foundation

Ahmanson Foundation

Annenberg Foundation

Eli & Edythe L. Broad Foundation

Cal National Bank

City of Los Angeles Cultural Affairs Department, Youth Arts and Education Program

Health Communications, Inc. (Chicken Soup for the Teenage Soul)

Liberty Hill Foundation – Donor Advised Fund

Los Angeles Times

Los Angeles Unified School District - Beyond the Bell Branch

Merrill Lynch

NBC/Universal Foundation

Oder Family Foundation

Open Meadows Foundation

Roth Family Foundation

RR Donnelley

Scarlett Letters

Soroptimist International of Los Angeles

Trailer Park

Wasserman Foundation

Weingart Foundation

The Women's Foundation of California – Athena Fund

Yahoo! Employee Foundation

It is clear that the power of one person's good idea, in concert with dedicated imaginative supporters can really go a long way!

Individuals (a partial list)

Anonymous
Barbara Abercrombie
Gillian Abercrombie
Stephanie Allen
Ronald & Carmen Anderson
Sara Apelkvist & Trevor St. John
Barbara & Jon Avnet
Scott Bairstow
Brenda Battista
Mark Bisgeier
Bob and Maxine Brauer
Janie Chavers
Barbara Corday
Elizabeth Craft
Ann Daniel
Bill Deegan
Kristina Deutsch & Joel Brand
Suzanne Dunaway
Fielding Edlow
Scott Einbinder
Denise Emanuel
Kimberly Emerson
Diane English & Joel Shukovsky
Sarah Fain
Maya Forbes
Betty Garrett
Jennie Garth
Jim Gauer
Gail Gilchrest
Sarah Goldfinger
Kathryn Grody
Elizabeth Forsythe Hailey
Cynthia Harrington
Lois & Dixon Harwin
Karen Heimberg
Angela Howard
Felicity Huffman
Margaret Hyde
Laurence Jacobson
May Jacobson
Karen Jantzen

Monica Karo
Deana E. Katz
Tammy Kaitz & Steve Crane
Alyson & Lawrence H. Krasner
Mary Leslie
Georgianne Levangie & Brian Grazer
Andrew Loo
Christina Lynch
Susan Lyne
John & Sandi Marshall
Dangene McKay-Bailey
Diana Meehan & Gary Goldberg
Anne Meredith
Kelly Merryman
Theresa Mulligan
Kathy Najimy
Jan Nash
Maria del Pilar O'Cadiz
Cilda Shaur O'Donnell
Lori and Frank Obregon
Marcia Paonessy
JJ Philbin
Aimee Pitta
Deborah Reber
Bill Resnick
Ilene Resnick
Nancy Morgan Ritter
Diane Siegel
Dana Spencer
Kristina Stanier
Michelle Steffes
Eva Stern
Jacques Henri Taylor
Allison Thomas
Beegie Truesdale
Nia Vardalos
Lynn Wasserman
Joan Stein Weiant
John & Marilyn Wells
Bud Yorkin

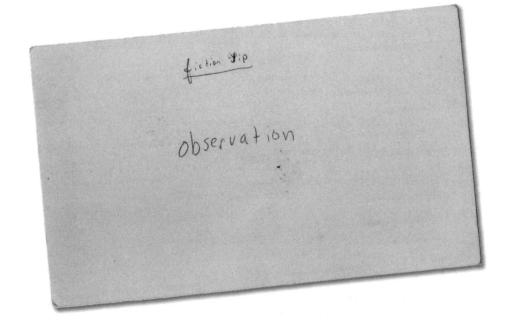

fiction tip
_____

observation

I am literally buzzing with excitement from
the creative energy that is WriteGirl.

In-Kind Contributors

All of us at WriteGirl thank the following for generously supporting our program and membership throughout the season:

For writing journals: **BrushDance Inc., Cavallini Papers & Co, Chronicle Books, Falling Water, Fiorentina, The Flavia Company, Galison/MudPuppy Press, K. Schweitzer, Kikkerland, New York Times, Peaceable Kingdom** and **Quotable Inc.**

Food, desserts and beverages at WriteGirl workshops and special events:
A & B Foods, Amazing Catering, Baja Fresh, Border Grill/Ciudad, Bristol Farms, Buddha's Belly, California Pizza Kitchen, Damon & Pythias, Davalan Sales, Cecilia Hae Jin Lee, Costco, The Farm in Beverly Hills, Island's, Fiji Water, Mijare's Mexican Restaurant, Louise's Trattoria, Modern Spirits, Noah's New York Bagels, Le Pain Quotidien, Panda Inn, POMWonderful, Susina Bakery, Whole Foods, and **Wildflower Baking Company**

Gifts for volunteers and girls: **Joanna Craft, Richard Foos and The Shout Factory, Rita Stafford and Up In Arms**

Printing and copy services: **Charisma Printing, Copy and Print Factory, Copy Page, Staples,** and **Wright Graphics**

Classic Party Rentals for dishware, glassware, and silverware

Creative City Café for a meeting space to brainstorm and plan

Councilman Eric Garcetti and **Councilman Tom LaBonge** (Los Angeles City Council) for support and acknowledgement of WriteGirl's contributions to the community

Fabric Interactive (www.fabricinteractive.com) and **Sara Apelkvist** for design and branding strategy, including development of WriteGirl's logo, website, press kit, stationery, publications and ongoing support

Los Angeles Times Festival of Books and **West Hollywood Book Fair** for donating WriteGirl booth space and promotional support at these events

Jacques Taylor and **BioConstructs** (www.bioconstructs.com) for ongoing support

UCLA Extension Writer's Program for assistance in recruiting mentors and volunteers for WriteGirl through their faculty and student populations

Marge Tebankin for guidance and support

Wendy Tigerman for graphic design skills

Yucca Community Center for providing a space where over 150 women and girls gather to write

Meet The WriteGirl Mentors

Susan Abram is a reporter for the *Los Angeles Daily News*, where she covers county issues. She has written stories for the *Los Angeles Times* and *LA Weekly*, and has worked as a reporter in Connecticut and New York.

Maia Akiva is a philosophy writer. Her plays have been trying to find the meaning of life without any success so far. She is currently working on her first novel, "The Human Happiness Campaign."

Stephanie Allen is a mother, surfer, writer, artist and actress, who currently holds a day job as a marketing executive at Fox Searchlight Pictures. Stephanie is putting the finishing touches on a collection of short fiction and poetry and has completed her seventh screenplay.

Abby Anderson hails from Canada, where she worked in the film industry. Abby is a screenwriter whose last two scripts made it to the Second Round of Austin Film Festival's screenplay and teleplay competitions.

Melissa Anderson Sweazy is a Los Angeles screenwriter, columnist and newlywed.

Marna Bunger, working with Fortune 100 companies, government, nonprofits, small businesses, startups and agencies, has more than 15 years of senior-level marketing and communications success. She finds humor in her own life and beyond as the creative force behind dontmincewords.com.

Tracy Chait is finishing her graduate degree in English at Middlebury College this year and is also a freelance writer who focuses on philanthropy and L.A. culture. She thinks WriteGirl is the greatest thing since pen and paper.

Catherine Cook is a warrior poet still warming up her pen. She is currently editing her first children's novel, working on a screenplay, and writing odes for the interesting people she encounters. She has a B.A. in English and teaches for LAUSD.

M. Irene Daniel, aside from being an attorney and first-time novelist, is a Desert Rat. She was born and raised in a tiny rural community in central Arizona, but moved to Los Angeles to attend law school at UCLA. She now resides with her husband and two cats in Eagle Rock, California.

Sue Davis is a writer of fascinating copy for a large insurance company by day, freelance articles by night and blogs about food and life whenever she gets a chance.

Jennifer Dohr teaches English and creative writing at Harvard-Westlake School in Los Angeles. She writes fiction for children and young adults.

Denise Emanuel belongs to the women's writing/performance group, Literary Stew. She recently received an award in a contest sponsored by American Pen Women, and has a story in the *Georgetown Review*. She's in the Writers' Program at UCLA Extension.

Geraldine Farrell's latest project, *DRUMMIN' UP PEACE*, a one-act play on conflict resolution, is touring Southern California schools. Her award-winning one-woman show, *BEATRICE*, has been seen on stage and heard on radio throughout the United States and Canada.

Hilary Galanoy is a feature-film screenwriter who has written projects for MGM, Paramount, Universal, Disney and New Regency. She's also a devotee of Ashtanga Yoga and a whiz at the barbecue.

Kate Gale writes librettos, poetry and fiction. She is the Managing Editor of Red Hen Press and the Editor of the *Los Angeles Review*. She teaches creative writing in the Graduate Humanities Program at Mount St. Mary's.

Elizabeth Gill is a screenwriter who enjoys writing fiction and poetry. Her credits include television movies, as well as the series *My So-Called Life*. She teaches screenwriting at USC and UCLA Extension, and is the mother of two grown daughters.

Karen Girard, originally from the fierce woods of rural Massachusetts, is a poet and writer with a Ph.D. from Stanford. Her works include children's workbooks and educational booklets. She loves running and is currently working on her first novel.

Jessica Goldstein has written for several TV sitcoms, pilots, an awards show and a kids' show. She is a foot shorter than her writing partner, Chrissy.

T. Faye Griffin is a veteran TV pen-for-hire whose credits include *The Parent 'Hood* and the Emmy Award-winning comedy series, *In Living Color*. Her work has appeared in numerous publications such as *Woman's World Magazine* and the *Los Angeles Times*.

Erika Hayasaki is a reporter for the *Los Angeles Times* who covers kids and education. She has won the *Los Angeles Times* "Best Writing" Award for her stories about a new teacher's plight, a boy's dangerous journey to earn an education and a cultural divide on a Latino campus. In 2006, she was a recipient of the American Society of Newspaper Editors prize for team deadline news reporting for the coverage of a train crash in Glendale, California.

Lexa Houska is in her third season with WriteGirl and writes about underpants for Frederick's of Hollywood. It is very sexy and glamorous. Jealous?

Jennifer Hoppe has ridden the bucking film trade for a decade. Currently, she has a TV project in development with Paramount and, in addition, Ridley Scott's company is producing a script she and her partner wrote last year.

Dominique Howard is an avid fiction and creative nonfiction writer with a love for life, friends and international travel. Dominique holds a degree in Business Administration from Florida A&M University and enjoys sharing the gift of the written word with the next generation of female writers.

Shannon Johnson-Haber is the Director of Communications for the Los Angeles Unified School District, Facilities Services Division. She oversees all public relations strategies for the division's $14 billion new school construction and modernization program. Shannon also loves to write poetry.

Erica Jon Kelly is a law clerk and media consultant by day and a law student at Southwestern University, School of Law at night. She is inspired daily by music, mayhem and margaritas.

New York singer/songwriter, **Michelle Lewis**, has written songs for many well-known artists (such as Cher, Shawn Colvin and Michelle Branch) in addition to releasing her own albums. She has recently created a kid's TV show about music, which is in development with Disney.

Kelly Merryman, originally from Texas, is in business development at Sony Pictures. She strives to decrease her time spent creating PowerPoint presentations and increase her time devoted to writing.

Theresa Mulligan is a television comedy writer. Her credits include *The Loop, Greetings from Tucson, Run of the House, Method & Red* and *South Park*. She's originally from the Midwest and has a cat named Frank and a man named Jeff.

Sandra O'Briant's work has appeared in *Café Irreal, Best Lesbian Love Stories of 2004, Women Write the Southwest,* and *Latinos in Lotus Land. Excerpts from The Secret of Old Blood: The Sandoval Sisters*, have appeared in *La Herencia, FriGG,* and *The Copperfield Review*. Her book reviews have been published on *La Bloga* and *Moorishgirl*. Please visit her at www.sramosobriant.com.

Carolina Paiz is a Guatemalan writer who lives in Los Angeles with her husband, Diego Velasco. Her short fiction has appeared in *Zoetrope* and the *Caribbean Writer*. She currently works as a staff writer for *Grey's Anatomy*.

Cece Peri holds a doctorate in psychology. She is a poet and research writer. Her poems have appeared in various journals, including *Speechless*, and the *San Gabriel Valley Poetry Quarterly*. In 2006, she was awarded the first Anne Silver Poetry Award.

Alix K. Pham is a screenwriter and poet. Her first screenplay, Skin, is being shopped around by producers. She is currently working on her second screenplay, Forever, an intense drama about co-dependence and alcoholism.

Kimberly Minten Purcell is the celebrity interviewer for the popular PBS tween website, *It's My Life*, and is currently working on two young adult thrillers.

Marietta Putignano King is currently editing her first novel, working on a screenplay and a one-act. In addition to being an actress, she is also a personal trainer and a painter. She currently studies dancing and Italian.

Teresa Rochester is an award-winning reporter for the Ventura County Star. She is a firm believer that truth is funnier and stranger than fiction. This was Teresa's first year with WriteGirl and it has left her in awe and inspired.

Faryl Saliman Reingold's colorful background includes medical writing, entertainment journalism, and production coordinating six Oscars broadcasts. She holds a Master's from USC and has authored a lifestyle manual and website to help people with spinal cord injuries avoid pressure sores.

Jayna Rust is an eighth grade language arts teacher and Teach For America corps member. She graduated from MU's School of Journalism while working as a sports reporter. She is now beginning her return to journalism.

Fabiola Sandoval is the asset manager for Esperanza Community Housing Corporation, managing the agency's policy to develop and preserve affordable housing. She writes for a small community paper and enjoys all-around creative cross-movement building.

Stephanie Schneider is a native Californian who loves living near the beach. She is the Director of Public Relations at a Foster Family & Adoption Agency. She enjoys working with youth and is an avid sports fan, especially of her alma mater's team, the UCLA Bruins.

Colleen Sharkey is a science writer and public-outreach coordinator for NASA's Jet Propulsion Laboratory. She graduated from the University of Cincinnati with a B.A. in English literature and is currently writing a master's thesis on the spoof newspaper, *The Onion*.

Jill Sheffield is a graduate of Sarah Lawrence College and recently received an M.F.A. in writing for children and young adults from Vermont College. She has been a copywriter for many years and writes funny, magical realism young adult novels.

Diane Siegel is a Museum Educator and writer currently working with intriguing objects and wonderful volunteers at the Pasadena Museum of History. She is proud to be a founding advisory board member of WriteGirl.

Shauna Smith works in the Organic Foods industry by day, but after hours, you'll find her dancing, performing and teaching salsa dance. She writes poetry and short non-fiction, and has been with WriteGirl for three years.

Amaree Tanawong has been a mentor with WriteGirl for the last three seasons. She is currently a technical writer/mergers and acquisition consultant at Ernst and Young. Amaree will be returning to school in the Fall in order to pursue an MBA.

Katherine Taylor earned her M.F.A. at Columbia University, where she was a Graduate Writing Fellow. She has won a Pushcart Prize and a McGinnis-Ritchie Award for Fiction. Her first novel and collection of stories are forthcoming.

Wendy Tigerman has counseled teens in NYC, raised alfalfa sprouts in Berkeley, and written everything from award-winning ad copy to *The Pink Panther* cartoons. Current projects: an indie film, a memoir class and a children's book with her husband Gary.

Pam Turski's writing runs the gamut from the random to the commonplace. She has created copy for advertising firms, scripts for televised serials, and press materials for the famous and nearly so. She is awed and inspired by WriteGirl.

When **Dana Valenzuela** isn't writing a press release, a media alert or a corporate biography for one her clients, she's dreaming of someday writing something longer than three pages. She hopes it might bring a few laughs.

Sarah Vance received an MFA in Film Production from the University of Southern California. Prior to film school, she wrote and produced radio and television commercials. Currently, she works as a staff reporter for a weekly entertainment trade publication.

Melissa Carolus Verlet has worked in journalism and education. She teaches history at the Archer School for Girls in Brentwood. She was a 2002–2003 Fulbright Fellow in France and is finishing her dissertation in European History at UCLA.

Joan Watson-Patko has an MSW from Temple University. As the Community Trainer at the Downtown Women's Center she trains staff members of agencies in the Skid Row area, writes grants, and creates educational materials and service manuals. WriteGirl has given her the means to bring more creativity into her writing.

Marlys West was a Hodder Fellow at Princeton University, an NEA grant recipient in poetry, and received an M.F.A. from the Michener Center for Writers. Akron Press published her book of poems, *Notes for a Late-Blooming Martyr*, in 1999.

Stacy N. Williams is a high school English teacher in the Los Angeles Unified School District. She is also a recent graduate of the University of Southern California's Master of Professional Writing program.

Ashley Wilson writes screenplays and works as a script analyst for Film Independent, the Expo and individual producers. When not at her computer, she can be found hiking or on a tennis court.

Rachel Wimberly has spent a lifetime just figuring out how to write about anything, anytime, anywhere. In her quest she has lived in 9 states and 3 foreign countries and written for CNN, the New York Times Regional Newspapers, *Variety Magazine* and *Scr(i)pt Magazine,* among others.

Index by Author

About the Editor and WriteGirl Leadership

Keren Taylor is the founder and Executive Director of WriteGirl. Passionate about inspiring others to cultivate their creative ideas, Keren has conducted hundreds of creative writing workshops for both youth and adults in Los Angeles and New York City. She has also led staff development workshops on literacy programming for the California Department of Education, LA's BEST, the YWCA, the New York Partnership for Afterschool Education, and the Children's Creative Writing Campaign. Her poetry has

appeared in many literary journals as well as *So Luminous the Wildflowers – An Anthology of California Poetry* from Tebot Bach Press. Keren has performed her original music across the country in concert halls, theatres, clubs and festivals with her a capella vocal group, *The Trembles,* and as a solo artist. She has opened for such acts as *Blood, Sweat & Tears, Marvin Hamlisch, Dana Carvey, Frank Sinatra Junior* and *Gladys Knigh*t. Keren spent a year in Las Vegas as a featured act at the New York New York Hotel & Casino. She is also a visual artist working mostly with paper and found objects, and the cover of Untangled is one of her original assemblages. From Vancouver, Canada, Keren Taylor now lives in Los Angeles with her husband, Jacques Henri Taylor, and their chocolate lab, Wasabi.

Allison Deegan serves as WriteGirl's Associate Director and as a member of the Advisory Board. Professionally, she is a business writer and consultant with more than 20 years of experience counseling clients on communications, marketing, organizational management, venture capital, public affairs and business development. Currently, she is Business Advisory Services Manager for the Los Angeles County Office of Education, where she works on school district management and governance. She holds a degree in Marketing from Syracuse University and is pursuing a graduate degree in Public Policy and Administration at California State University, Long Beach. Her creative activities include screenwriting and poetry, which she works on with her WriteGirl mentee.

Phoebe Brauer serves as WriteGirl's Program Coordinator. She joined the organization in 2005 and focuses on program development, publications and mentoring management. She is also part of the core staff for WriteGirl's Destiny Academy project in South Los Angeles. A native Angeleno, Phoebe is a graduate of Georgetown University's Walsh School of Foreign Service in Washington, DC. She has worked overseas on children's service projects and as an editor for academic, literary, art and cross-cultural publications. She appreciates the opportunity to work with and learn from two dedicated and driven women, Keren and Allison.

About WriteGirl Publications

Since 2001, WriteGirl Publications has been publishing award-winning anthologies that showcase the bold voices and imaginative insights of women and girls. Unique in both design and content, WriteGirl anthologies present a wide range of personal stories, poetry, essays, scenes and lyrics, as well as a selection of WriteGirl writing "experiments" to inspire readers to find their own creative voices.

Other Publications by WriteGirl

Nothing Held Back: Truth and Fiction from WriteGirl
Pieces of Me: The Voices of WriteGirl
Bold Ink: Collected Voices of Women & Girls
Threads
Look at Me Long Enough: Creative Writing from the Girls of Destiny Academy

About WriteGirl

WriteGirl is a creative writing and mentoring organization that pairs professional women writers with teen girls. Through one-on-one mentoring, monthly workshops, public readings and publications, WriteGirl's innovative writing program offers girls techniques and insights in all genres of writing, from poetry to journalism to fiction and more. WriteGirls support, encourage and challenge each other to express themselves, their ideas and dreams on paper and out loud. Through involvement in the WriteGirl program and community of writers, girls develop communication and life skills, self-confidence, self-esteem and an expanded view of themselves and their futures. WriteGirl, a project of nonprofit organization Community Partners, was founded in December 2001 in Los Angeles.

WriteGirl welcomes your support and involvement:
Visit WriteGirl on the web at www.writegirl.org